put off thy shoes

A JOURNEY THROUGH PALESTINE

by Elizabeth Hamilton

A Catholic and a classicist, Elizabeth Hamilton makes of this journey a moving spiritual experience. She can evoke landscape and atmosphere with magical precision; travelling through Israel and Jordan, she conveys vividly both the holy places and the modern world of *kibbutzim* and of an Arab refugee camp. Here are Jerusalem and the Old City, Tel Aviv, Jaffa, Nazareth, Caesarea, Bethlehem, Petra, and many more aspects of Palestine.

A vivid travel book, PUT OFF THY SHOES is also much more. The depth and substance come in part from Miss Hamilton's knowledge of the past; they come from her reverent understanding of both Judaism and Islam. B[illegible] particularly distinguishes the [illegible] fact that it expresses a sensiti[illegible] foundly Christian spirit, and [illegible] simplicity and truth.

PUT OFF THY SHOES

ELIZABETH HAMILTON

Put Off Thy Shoes

A JOURNEY THROUGH PALESTINE

CHARLES SCRIBNER'S SONS

NEW YORK

A. 12-57 [MH]

Printed in the United States of America

LIBRARY OF CONGRESS CATALOG CARD NUMBER. 57-12357

CONTENTS

ILLUSTRATIONS

To

Peter Abu Nasser and Abdullah

at Nazareth

'It is called Holy Land, firstly, for having been so named by God, in the book of Exodus, the second Chapter, when He says to Moses: "Put off thy shoes from thy feet, for the place whereon thou standest is holy ground".'

A TREATISE ON THE HOLY LAND

Written for his sister by Friar Francesco Suriano in the year 1485.

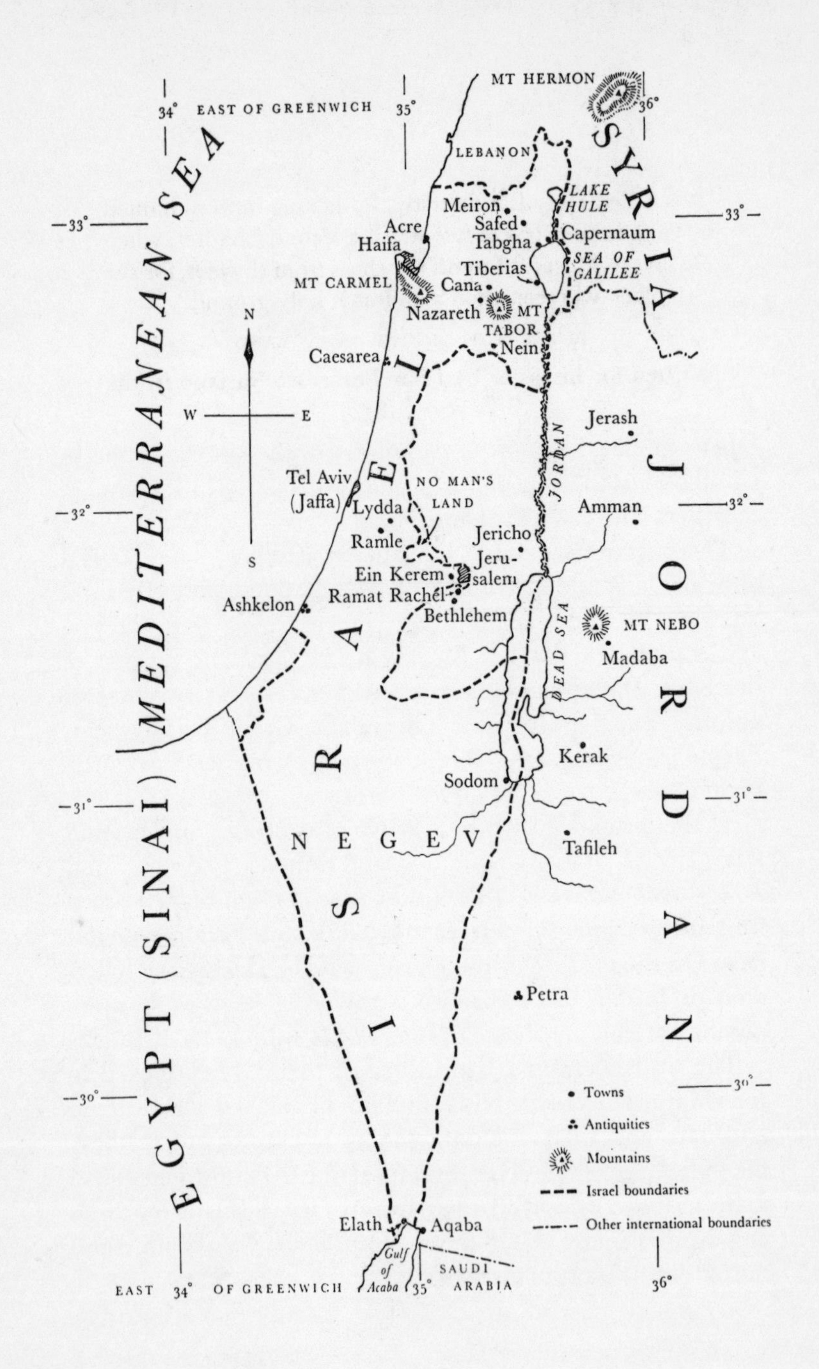

MT HERMON
34° EAST OF GREENWICH 35°
36°
MEDITERRANEAN SEA
EGYPT (SINAI)
LEBANON
SYRIA
ISRAEL
JORDAN
LAKE HULE
Meiron
Safed
Acre
Haifa
Capernaum
Tabgha
SEA OF GALILEE
Tiberias
MT CARMEL
Cana
Nazareth
MT TABOR
Nein
Caesarea
N
W
E
S
33°
Jerash
JORDAN
Tel Aviv (Jaffa)
Lydda
NO MAN'S LAND
Amman
32°
Ramle
Jericho
Jeru-salem
Ein Kerem
Ramat Rachel
Ashkelon
Bethlehem
MT NEBO
Madaba
DEAD SEA
Kerak
Sodom
31°
NEGEV
Tafileh
Petra
30°
Towns
Antiquities
Mountains
Israel boundaries
Other international boundaries
Elath
Aqaba
Gulf of Acaba
SAUDI ARABIA
EAST 34° OF GREENWICH 35°
36°

CHAPTER I

Jerusalem in Israel: I

I

JERUSALEM. The city of castellated walls known to me in childhood from Bible pictures. The city set on a hill: compact together. The city that Christ wept over.

There were date palms outside my window. They looked absurdly lank and naked, their tall cinnamon-coloured trunks tapering to a crown of silvery-green leaves that flapped and scraped in the hot breeze. Below, was the garden of the King David Hotel, massed with trees and shrubs and flowers. Eucalyptus trees. Oleanders. Great prickly-pear. Purple bougainvillea. Sunflowers. Rosemary. Lavender. Snapdragons.

At the far end there was a hedge of cypresses and beyond this a stretch of dusty no man's land that reached away and up towards the walls of the Old City. The sun blazed down from a hard blue sky, turning the walls to a dazzling whiteness. On the far side of these walls was the Hashemite Kingdom of Jordan. To the south a quivering haze hung upon mountains that are the beginning of the wilderness of Judah.

The walls were as I had imagined them. They looked in the shimmering light, with the blue of the sky above them and here and there the dark shapes of cypress trees, like a magnification of one of those pictures that decorate a medieval manuscript. Yet, for all their beauty, there was a hardness and stubbornness about them. 'Jerusalem, Jerusalem, thou that killest the prophets. . . .'

I knew that if I were to see nothing else but the walls, nothing besides, the journey had been worth while. I had driven that morning from Lydda Airport in the mysterious hour that precedes the dawn. Great stars hung close to the earth. There was an elusive, haunting smell of herbs and soil not rained upon. Oleander blossoms showed scarlet and white in the headlights of the car. From time to time box-like houses seemed to leap out of the darkness. Then the stars faded. The sky became a sudden sheet of gold above hills terraced and clear-cut and red as blood. Cocks crowed. With no less suddenness the gold gave place to blue and under its brightness the red of the hills paled. I had supposed that the first sight of Jerusalem would be dramatic, breath-taking. It was not so. The pale stone houses with balconies and shutters, the wide streets, lined with trees and empty in the early morning, were pleasant. But that was all. Something I had expected was not there: I felt cheated. Then, from the window of my room, I saw the walls.

I slept through the heat of the day, dreaming in snatches. I was back in the aeroplane, watching the Jews saying their prayers. They had stood in the gangway, their bodies swaying, their voices rising and falling. They wore black skull-caps, and one of them supported himself against the luggage-rack, his head bowed. It was the Ninth day of Ab, a schoolboy at my side had told me: they were mourning the destruction of the Temple. . . . Then it seemed to me that it was raining and I was in the schoolroom of my childhood on a wet Irish afternoon. I opened my eyes. What I had taken for rain was the flapping and the scraping of the palm leaves, one against the other in the breeze. I slept again. When I woke, a veil of gold was hanging upon the walls and the tower of the Dormition church rising above them. The gold turned to rose, and the rose to crimson: the mountains of Judah were crimson, and the mountains of Moab were a haze of lilac that melted into the darkening sky.

* * *

I went downstairs and sat on the terrace drinking orange juice with Michael A. who had called from the Israel Foreign Office. His good-natured face smiled across at me in the half-light. '*Shalom! Shalom!* Welcome to Israel!' he said.

Welcome to Israel! That was what they all said. The official in white uniform at the airport. The two representatives from the Government Tourist Office. The woman who had driven up in a great khaki car eager to arrange a tour of hospitals and schools: she belonged, she explained, to a Jewish-American organization called Hadassah.

Welcome to Israel! The words had come over on the telephone before I had finished breakfast. The citizens of the new Israel are warm in their welcome to visitors. They want to talk, exchange ideas, hear impressions. . . . At that moment, Israel was represented by alert-looking men and women sitting on the terrace of the hotel, drinking fruit juice and talking in loud eager voices. Many of the men wore short-sleeved nylon shirts cut in the American style. The women were in printed cottons, some of them backless, almost all without sleeves.

There was nothing specifically Jewish in the appearance of these people. But, then, one of the first things I learnt in Israel was that there is no such thing as the 'typical Jew'. Each one bears the stamp of that part of the globe in which he, or his forbears, has lived; to the ways of which he has become adapted; or, if there is no adaptation, persecution has left a yet deeper mark.

In the new Israel Jews of the Diaspora have been ingathered from over seventy nations. In the Orthodox quarter of

Jerusalem the Jew whose forefathers lived in the mid-European ghetto is pale-faced; his eyes look to the ground; sometimes his shoulders are crouched; he wears side-curls, a kaftan, and a flat fur hat. There seems little in common between him and the smart modern-looking Jews who sit in the King David Hotel or walk up and down Ben Yehuda Street; or the sun-bronzed giants of the *kibbutzim*, the communal settlements, of which I shall say more. No, the variety between Jews is as between the nations of the world. In Jerusalem you will meet the Jew from, perhaps, Liverpool, speaking his English with a flat north-country accent. You will meet the Pole, the red-headed Scot, the soft-voiced Irishman. The Cochin Jew, who comes from India, might be a Malayan; his complexion is golden-brown, his hair straight and black, his eyes the shape of almonds. The immigrants from Iraq, squatting in doorways near the Mandelbaum Gate, have dark skins and frizzy hair. Those from Morocco are North Africans. The small slender Yemenite has a narrow face, high cheek-bones, an expression of gentle melancholy and an especial dignity of carriage. The Yemenites came to Israel from the furthest corner of Arabia, believing the aeroplanes which brought them to be the eagles promised by God to his holy people.

What is it, then, that makes one all these from so many nations – gives to them a distinction peculiarly their own? What is it that makes the Jew? I asked myself this question while I was in Israel. I asked Jews as well, yet without finding a complete answer.

Religion, some told me: the religion revealed alone to the Jews. Faith in one God, handed down from Abraham and Isaac and Jacob. The Talmud. The Torah. With the scrolls of the Law in their arms, Jews went to their death in the gas-chambers of Hitler. Yet the religious answer is not as simple as that. Thousands of Jews have abandoned religion as practised by their forefathers. These may respect Orthodoxy, but it has little relation to their lives. At its worst it is a burden of taboos and impositions standing in the way of progress and freedom. 'We are not religious', many a Jew in a *kibbutz* will tell you. For him the synagogue, the Sabbath, the hundred and one implications of the Law, have ceased to have meaning. For the Zionist (there are exceptions) religion is seen in terms of the re-birth of Israel: it has become nationalistic rather than theo-centric. A Utopia rather than a Messiah is his dream. Yet, it is a dream inspired by the Bible. For one thing all Jews share, whether they come from Europe or Africa, India or the Yemen, whether Orthodox or Unorthodox, is a deep respect for the Bible. They share, too, a belief in their destiny as a chosen people.

II

Dum medium silentium tenerent omnia. THE ROMAN BREVIARY

It was midnight. The city walls were washed to a dead, flat whiteness in the light of the moon, and cypress trees were black, and pointed as daggers. Across the walls a shaft of silver shone on the roof of the Holy Sepulchre. The croaking of frogs broke upon the silence. Far away a jackal howled. A cock began to crow: a sad, unsubstantial note, echoing back to the first Good Friday.

III

I came out of the church into the brightness of the morning. There were children on the steps wearing blue cotton dresses and heavy clattering shoes. They shouted to one another in high-pitched voices. A nun with bunchy skirts and a clinking rosary tried to gather them about her, ineffectually, like a flustered hen.

The sun shone, but the day was still cool.

I walked downhill along a dusty road with a high wall on one side. The sky was blue above the whiteness of the wall and the silver-grey of olive trees. On the other side there was a patch of waste ground where goldfinches fluttered above withered grasses. There are many such patches in Jerusalem: some have never been built on, others are the result of devastation during the fighting against the Arabs. Whatever the cause, they give a feeling of space. You can forget that a few minutes away there are shops and motor cars, buses and cinemas and crowded pavements.

A Franciscan went by, pink complexioned and tonsured – his brown habit fastened with a white knotted girdle, sandals on his feet. Then, a young Jew in an open-necked shirt, a brief-case under his arm. I passed the enormous building belonging to the Y.M.C.A. Its tower made me think of Westminster Cathedral. A Greek priest was coming out; his bearded face under the black, funnel-shaped head-dress had a secretive expression. A tussore sunshade hung from his arm.

I crossed the road to the King David Hotel. The great pillared lounge decorated in blue and green in a Biblical tradition was cool and quiet. Some American women sat at a table in readiness for an outing. They wore sun-glasses and carried expensive-looking cameras. Then, into the dining room for breakfast. A waiter in a white coat drew out a chair. His yellow-skinned face with the drooping eyelids had calm and dignity; it was the face of a Chinese.

CHAPTER II

Jerusalem in Israel: II

I

IN THE Orthodox quarter of Jerusalem beggars sit on the pavement. They are not cringing fellows – not the genuine ones among them. They want alms, of course, but they hold that they, too, have something to give. They give, in fact, their prayers. There they sit, their lips moving, a book open in front of them. The prayers are not for the donor personally, but for the Jewish people the world over – their needs and suffering. They are beggars with self-respect, labourers worthy of their hire.

I went through narrow streets, then under a tunnel-like gateway into a courtyard. In front was a great block of flats, built of brick and grim as a fortress. Railed balconies, one above the other, ran the length of the building. From it another tunnel-like gateway led into a second courtyard with a similar block of flats and yet another gateway. The three gateways were 'out of line', so that in the event of an attack there would be no direct way through.

Mea Shearim was built at the end of the last century to give homes to Jews from Europe. It is nearer in character to the ghetto of eastern Europe than to Jerusalem. Old people came here, that they might die in the Holy City. Some brought their grandchildren.

It was the middle of the week, yet the synagogue was crowded. Pale-faced men wearing side-curls and fur hats sat in groups. They looked like bats, I thought, in a sunless barn.

They were reading aloud from tattered books, or arguing and reasoning one with another. A murmur of voices rose. There were hard, twisted faces – as of people driven to protect themselves by craft or guile – but faces, too, lit with serenity. There were boys among them, putting in questions, then waiting in deference upon the answers of their elders.

'Are they here all day?' I asked my companion, himself a Jew. 'How do they earn a living?'

'They are rabbis and scholars and students,' he told me. 'They study the law in all its manifold interpretations – all the ramifications of the law and the commentaries upon it. Some have employment to eke out a living. The majority give their lives to this. Religion is their life.'

We walked through courtyards, under archways. Washing hung on lines and there was a smell of cooking and drains. A flight of outside steps led up to a balcony with the classrooms of a Talmudic school opening on to it. In one room a rabbi was reading from a yellow-leaved book. A glass of tea stood on the table at his side. Little boys with side-curls and skull-caps sat opposite him on benches, repeating his words, like an incantation, in monotonous sing-song voices. In another room there were older boys. One was interpreting a point of the law: his face was bright with intelligence, and a smile played on the lips of his master. In another, the children had been left on their own, and, like all children, were making the most of it. They were out of their places, and there was suppressed laughter. At the sight of us they were back on their benches in a flash, their heads bent, their lips moving. Then one head was raised and black, mischievous eyes stole a glance into my own.

We went down the stairs past a public wash-house and out into a street crowded with booths selling vegetables and fruit. In a shop that was hardly more than a hole in a wall, a woman was chasing a squawking fowl. Another sat milking a goat on the pavement. In the middle of it all, among pale-faced men and boys wearing stockings that covered their knees, a sun-tanned youth was painting at an easel. He wore a singlet and a pair of bright blue shorts characteristic of the *kibbutz* worker: his strong bare legs were burnt a deep mahogany.

'It's hard to reconcile the two,' I said. 'The young man in the shorts and the pale-faced Jews with the curls. Each seems to have something the other has not. It would be a pity to lose either.'

'Yes,' my companion answered thoughtfully. 'Each has something the other has not. The new Israel is very new and Orthodox Jewry is very old. A compromise must be found . . . that each may give of its best to the other.'

II

'*Remember the Sabbath day, to keep it holy.*' EXODUS

It was Friday evening. The eve of the Sabbath. The mood was one of preparation; a waiting on things to come.

The people of Mea Shearim live for the Sabbath. Sunday, Monday and Tuesday are the days after the Sabbath; Wednesday, Thursday and Friday, the days before it. The Sabbath is the crown of the week. It is, too, a symbol and foretaste of a future promised to the Children of Israel in the providence of God. For the Sabbath, the family come together: the father, the mother, the children – all who are of the household. On this day a husband addresses his wife as *Malkah*, which means queen.

There was no traffic in the streets of Mea Shearim. Only a ceaseless tread of feet. . . . Many of the men wore the fur hat that, from being the mark of shame in the ghettos of eastern

Europe, has become the pride of Orthodoxy. Boys wore similar hats or little satin skull-caps embroidered with flowers or with the star of David.

On a balcony young men, holding open books in their hands, stood with eyes turned to the west, waiting the moment of the sunset. Lamps glowed in doorways, and candles burnt behind barred windows.

We went from synagogue to synagogue, through a tangle of streets, up flights of steps, through cobbled courtyards, past shabby houses that yet had a lingering elegance.

As I went into one synagogue, I was given a sprig of rosemary. I stood at the back, the rosemary in my hand, watching. Near me votive candles were burning as in a Catholic church. At the far end bearded rabbis in rich embroidered robes sat side by side – as impassive as those Roman elders upon whom the barbarian Gauls, overcome with awe, dared not lay their hands in violence.

Then a young rabbi began to read aloud. His hair was a deep shining auburn and his face calm and beautiful in the lamplight, like the face of Christ in the work of an Old Master. Presently, a white-robed judge of the rabbinical courts gave notice that he would receive any men visitors. My Jewish escort and two Americans who were with us went forward and were shaken by the hand: it would have been defilement to take the hand of a woman. 'We all have one destination,' I heard the rabbi say, 'but our roads are different'.

The Persian synagogue was full of little old men with lined and rugged faces. They were beautiful, I thought, as old trees are beautiful. They sat there, cross-legged, on cushions covered in gay striped materials. Some wore white socks, but most were bare-foot. It is their custom to leave their shoes outside, for, while living under Moslem domination before coming to Israel, they had adopted Moslem ways; just as, in medieval Spain,

Jews took over Catholic customs, conforming outwardly to the country's faith, but secretly practising their own.

The little Yemenite synagogue had a white vaulted roof and walls hung with yellow. Men with large dark eyes sat on a blue and red carpet, their heads and shoulders swathed in black and white. They prayed with deep concentration, in strange wild tones, swaying their bodies. Their manner of worship is born of their life of persecution. In the Yemen they were debarred by their Moslem overlords from mounting a camel: it was unfitting that a Jew be higher above the ground than a Moslem. On the Sabbath, however, in the shelter of their synagogue they were able to give rein to their pent-up longings, employing, in their address to God, the rhythms and movements that once they had used when riding camels in the desert.

We looked through the window of a Hassidic synagogue. Men in fur hats, their books open in front of them, stood praying in the candlelight. Their discordant voices merged into a melancholy harmony. Each prayed alone. Each addressed himself to his creator, pleading, arguing, lamenting, wringing his hands, waving his arms. I watched a young man. His eyes glowed. His body swayed. He gesticulated wildly, as though he were wrangling with God – as though he despaired of him, yet must, by some means, make him see the unreasonableness of his ways.

'Boy!' said one of the Americans. 'Another twenty years and there'll be none of this!'

'I'm not sure,' said the Jew. 'Tradition is strong.'

'Yep!' said the American thoughtfully. 'But what about progress?' He pronounced the word with a short 'o'.

'It doesn't make sense,' broke in the second American. 'The new Israel and the *kibbutz* boys and yet this?'

It was my problem over again.

'Israel is in the melting pot,' the Jew answered. 'We must have patience.'

The streets were dark now. Only candlelight in windows and, overhead, the stars. In a few minutes we were back among buses and motors, cafés and cinemas – all that the word progress suggested. In Jerusalem past is near to the present, things celestial to things terrestial.

I had known next to nothing about Jewish Orthodoxy. What I had seen left a deep impression. I questioned my companion. He answered me patiently, yet I could sense a hidden impatience. 'You can see this kind of thing in a city in Europe,' he said. 'You do not need to come to Jerusalem for it!' He would have been better pleased if I had asked him about the laying of the pipeline through the Negev.

* * *

I dined that night with the British Consul and his wife. We talked of books, horses, birds, gardens, the churches – both Anglican and Roman. I felt as though we were in England. Yet, from the balcony where we sat, I looked on to the walls of the Old City, pale under a sky that was thick with stars. They were the stars that I knew, but they shone with a greater brilliance, and the constellations were tilted at an unfamiliar angle. The walls entranced me. I was thinking of the day when I would see what it was they contained. I thought, too, of the Jews in Mea Shearim, with their fur hats and their side-curls, keeping their Sabbath in their synagogues and candlelit homes; of the Yemenites sitting cross-legged on their carpet, and the bare-foot old men from Persia. I thought of the prosperous-looking Jews in the King David Hotel, many of them from the United States; then, of the Jews in the *kibbutzim*, few of them Orthodox, none of them prosperous. So many worlds were meeting.

CHAPTER III

Jerusalem in Israel: III

I

CHATEAUBRIAND described Mount Zion as being about as high as Montmartre, but rounder at the top. From a distance it looks as though it were enclosed in the walls of the Old City. In fact, it stands inside its own walls. Except for a short period, during Byzantine times, this has been so since Hadrian rebuilt Jerusalem after its destruction by the Emperor Titus in A.D. 70. Following the custom of the Romans, Hadrian wanted the city to be square; to achieve this he had to exclude the hills of Zion and Ophel that lie to the south.

Whether Mount Zion is the biblical Zion, the original city of King David, or whether the latter, as archeologists now say, was on the neighbouring Mount Ophel, is of little account. By long tradition the mount that is called Zion has become hallowed as the cradle of the city – a place that is holy beyond all others. Moreover, it is today the one part of the old Jerusalem that is still in Jewish hands. It was captured in the war of liberation, and some of the fiercest fighting took place on its heights. Under its dark archways candles burn in memory of the dead. They also burn in the tomb of David where there is a shrouded sarcophagus, and, resting on it, silver crowns and scroll cases. For the Jews Mount Zion is a symbol of the history of the children of Israel: it is a place on which to meditate on God's revelation to his Chosen People: on the sufferings of those people, and their salvation through the birth of a new Israel. From it, too, they look

down upon the Old City and the Wailing Wall from which they are debarred.

For the Christian, also, Mount Zion is a holy place. The pilgrims of old, approaching Jerusalem from Jaffa, used suddenly to see not the whole of the city but, as La Brocquière said, the part that adjoins Mount Zion and 'the holy Mount Zion itself, with all its buildings and ruins'. At the sight they would cry out for joy, and kneel and kiss the earth.

For, here, is the *Cenaculum*, the Upper Room that was the place of the Last Supper and the Coming Down of the Holy Spirit, with, below this, the room of the Washing of the Feet. Here, tradition says, was the house of John Mark, and it was here that Christ's Mother died. When the Romans destroyed Jerusalem, they spared this house, and the Christians, coming back from Pella, had their first church in it. In the fifteenth century the Franciscans rebuilt the room as it is now. The Gothic pillars and arches suggest an Italian painting of the Last Supper, rather than the Supper itself. For me, it was the simple flight of steps leading up to the room on the outside of the building that, more than anything else, brought to life the happenings of Maundy Thursday. Especially was this so at night, when darkness threw into relief the pale stone wall and the steps going up it, while, above, the stars glinted, and the breeze soughed in the pines.

II

Jerusalem in Israel is a modern city, yet hardly for a moment can you forget the past.

To the south, there is a road from which you look away beyond the wilderness, where David pastured his sheep, to the Dead Sea – with, across it, Mount Nebo, the traditional burial place of Moses.

Further along the road you come to Ramat Rachel, the Mount of Rachel. Rachel was buried almost in sight of Jerusalem: her white, domed tomb is on the road to Bethlehem, now in Jordan territory. During the war there was fierce fighting at Ramat Rachel. A wrecked building stands there, its walls pocked with bullets. There are Herodian excavations, and the remains of a Byzantine church, and, beyond these, the frontier.

I stood above a trench protected by sandbags and barbed wire, looking across at a great sweep of open country. Larks were singing. Only a few yards away, on the 'Other Side', a shepherd boy with a staff in his hand was tending a flock of black goats. To the east, above the serrated mountains of Judah, the cone-shaped Herodium rose ash-pale against the sky. To the west was the fortress-monastery of Saint Elijah. Ahead, I saw spires and belfries and fields that seemed almost to fringe the wilderness. It was Bethlehem. The fields were those in which Ruth reaped, and where the Shepherds saw the Angels. 'Bethlehem; Bethlehem; *Ce nom recommence à chanter*. . . .' There was something poignant about seeing Bethlehem from behind barbed wire.

CHAPTER IV

Ein Kerem

EIN KEREM is the birthplace of John the Baptist. It is four and a half miles from Jerusalem, among red, terraced hills. Its stucco houses and cypress trees, its flights of steps and narrow streets, its donkeys and dark-eyed children, make it like a hill-town in Italy. There is a well, where they tell you Christ's Mother drew water. But, as Père Roger said, there is no proof; enough that she lived for months in this countryside carrying within her the Incarnate Word of God.

A steep, stone-strewn path leads uphill to the church of the Visitation. Below, to the right, are vineyards and gardens and, beyond, hills planted on their lower slopes with olives and vines, then reaching away barren against the sky. On the left there is a Russian convent behind a high wall: a notice on the door gave warning of a savage dog. Above the wall I could see a nun gardening among the fruit trees.

Another nun passed on the road; she wore unrelieved black that came close about her face, and a cap going to a point like a knight's helmet. This head-dress, which is not confined to nuns, is said to have come down to the Russians from their Scythian ancestors.

The wrought-iron gates into the courtyard of the church of the Visitation were locked. Père Roger clanged a bell. A Franciscan brother looked out of a window, then came down, a key in his hand. One of the walls of the courtyard was decorated with plaques giving the Magnificat in different languages. There were oleander trees and, beyond the church and monastery, a garden full of shrubs and bright flowers.

The rock cavity underneath the church is, according to tradition, part of the house belonging to the priest Zachary, and the meeting place of Mary and her cousin Elizabeth. It is comparable to the cave of the Annunciation at Nazareth. There are families in the Middle East today living in caves, or in houses where the back is a cave to which a stone front has been added.

There is a second church at Ein Kerem dedicated to John the Baptist. It is approached by steps, then a vaulted porch in which a blind woman sat begging. In a chapel, a little below the level of the ground, a stone bears the words

'*Hic Precursor Domini natus est.*'

It may well be that John was born here – that Zachary, who was reputed to be a wealthy man, had two houses. Or perhaps the tradition of his birth in this place grew up from the fact that in early times there was a martyr's shrine near by. Red and black mosaics are preserved, going back to the Byzantine period – as well as oil-presses still stained from the green of the oil.

We sat under a carob tree in the garden belonging to the convent of Notre Dame de Zion – Mr Irron, Père Roger, and myself. Mr Irron was Jewish and dapper. Père Roger was a great big man with a gentle expression and feet that showed brown as an Indian's between the leather of his sandals. His black Assumptionist habit was faded to a streaky green. He was smoking a calabash pipe; when he smiled his gold-filled teeth glinted white above his black beard.

Presently he put his pipe away, and began picking up the carob pods that strewed the ground. He snapped one open and chewed the yellow seeds. The carob is also called the locust tree. The pods are used to feed animals. Some of them are as much as ten inches long. Because of their bent shape, the Greeks gave them the name *keration*, which means a little horn. These were the 'husks' on which the Prodigal Son fed. Sometimes the tree grows to an immense size, and has spreading foliage. An officer in the Israeli Army told me how, during the war of liberation, thirty of his men found shelter under a single tree.

Adjoining the convent garden there was a walled-in burial ground, full of the hot scent of pines. Cicadas grated and little bulbul birds called to one another gently. Here was the grave of Père Ratisbonne, a convert from Judaism and the founder of the nuns of Notre Dame de Zion. Père Roger knelt at the grave. 'Father Ratisbonne is buried here,' he said, 'and on the hill only a short way off is the grave of Herzl. Both of them great Jews, both servants of their people.' On the way from Jerusalem we had passed the tomb of Theodor Herzl, the man who planned and foretold the State of Israel fifty years before its birth.

A nun brought us in from the garden. Pomegranate wine in tall glasses was waiting for us in the parlour.

* * *

Mr Irron had asked us to lunch at his flat on the outskirts of Jerusalem. We stopped on the way to pick up some wine. Père Roger got out of the car to fetch it. He came back carrying a bottle hidden in each sleeve. His arms looked stiff and wooden, as if he were a Noah's Ark figure. We laughed.

'The sleeves of the church,' he said, laughing in turn, 'are big enough to hide the sins of the world'.

CHAPTER V

Tel Aviv

TEL AVIV is everything that Jerusalem is not.

Jerusalem, even modern Jerusalem, is a city born of her past, and her past is still with her. Tel Aviv is of today and tomorrow; she has no past. Where the city now stands, thirty years ago there was nothing – only the sea breaking on the edge of the desolate sand-dunes. Jerusalem is a planned city, built from the alabaster-coloured stone that is quarried on the spot. Tel Aviv is a higgle-piggle of buildings – hotels, blocks of flats, business houses, factories. Most of them are made of concrete and blatantly modern. They are flung there at random, one almost on top of another.

Jerusalem has dignity and calm, Tel Aviv is all rush and bustle. Jerusalem, even Jerusalem in Israel, remains a Christian city. There are monasteries and convents and churches. Mass is said. The place of the Last Supper is there. Tel Aviv is wholly Jewish. There are synagogues but no churches. Jerusalem has a gentle, lovely climate; hot, dry days, and nights that are cool even in the middle of summer. At Tel Aviv the enervating heat of the day gives place only to sticky suffocating nights. The people of Jerusalem, any Jew will tell you, live in their homes and entertain in them. In Tel Aviv they pass their time in cafés where they congregate till late at night, reading papers, gossiping with friends, discussing the theatre, the arts, and, above all, politics and the State of Israel. At night, the streets of Jerusalem are dark and quiet. In Tel Aviv shop windows are a blaze of light and pavements are crowded: there is music and dancing, there are night-clubs, and near by, perched above the dunes and the sea, is an hotel where the dance floor would vie with any in Europe.

Jerusalem held me captive: I had no wish to visit Tel Aviv. I was only persuaded into going there by the shocked protests of Jewish friends. 'You intend writing a book about Israel and you don't want to see Tel Aviv?' they exclaimed in justifiable dismay.

The Jew who lives in Jerusalem naturally prefers his city to Tel Aviv. Yet even he is proud of Tel Aviv. Tel Aviv stands for the new Israel, and, generally speaking, it is the new Israel that the Jew wants to show the visitor. He wants you to see hospitals, schools, clinics, settlements, research stations – as though to say, 'Look, what we can do! Look, what we have done!' His racial inferiority complex, conditioned by persecution, shows itself, as so often, in a pose of superiority. He blows his trumpet, and blows it loudly. This is understandable, for, he thinks to himself, if he does not blow it, who will? In the words of an ancient rabbi, he thinks: 'If I am not for myself, who will be for me?'

It was not surprising, then, that I should sense at times a hidden impatience because I showed more interest in the painted tomb at Ashkelon than in the newly built Ashkelon Afridar; in the Roman marbles at Caesarea than in the Weizmann Institute; in the tortoises of the Hule marshes than in the project to drain these marshes.

I spoke of this to a sympathetic listener.

'It has to be,' he said. 'We Zionists are pioneers. We have much to do, much to attend to. As your poet put it, we have "no time to stand and stare" – not yet.' Of course, I am generalizing. Israel has her naturalists, her poets, her artists and her archeologists. I remember a government official who

Sounding the *shofar* in a synagogue at the New Year.

Young men at a typical *kibbutz*

The Sea Wall of Acre

confessed to caring less about the *kibbutzim* than about the finds at Beitsha'an. General Moshe Dayan 'digs' in his spare time, and, because in Israel you can hardly disturb the soil without coming upon pottery or mosaic or marbles, it is not uncommon for a *kibbutz* to have a museum to display such treasures. . . . Yet, what must strike a newcomer is the consuming all-out activity concerning practical, material things.

Certainly Tel Aviv is no place to stand and stare. You are likely to be thrust off the pavement. But that again is only a half-truth. For when I did come to a stand in its streets, whether because I had lost my way, or in sheer bewilderment at the crowds and the din of voices talking a language that was unintelligible to me, someone was sure to confront me with an offer of help: I do not mean touting guides, but genuine, friendly people.

One of the things that puzzled me at first was the reiterated cry: '*Sherut! Sherut!*' The word means 'service' and is used of the communal taxis that are an inexpensive means of transport in both Israel and Jordan. They not only run in the towns, but are also a means of getting from one town to another. Provided you have a seat by a window, to travel by *sherut* is a pleasant way of seeing the country. In any case, it is an adventure: there is no knowing who your companions will be.

* * *

Restless and scurrying though Tel Aviv is, the city has another less obvious side which finds expression in the Boulevard Rothschild with its gardens and gracious houses. I remember an evening spent on the balcony of one of these. Below, the wide, quiet street was lined with trees that were vividly green in the lamplight. At the corner a blue kiosk sold magazines and newspapers. My hostess was a lawyer who played an important part in the life of the city; she would have been mayoress, she explained, had she not abandoned the idea because it did not please her schoolboy son. 'I am wife and mother first,' she said. She spoke with nostalgia of a visit to England, when she had moved among people interested in the problems and rights of women.

Her husband made me the more welcome because I was a Catholic. 'You will remember me,' he said, taking my hands into his, 'as the Jew who loves Lourdes. . . . Lourdes,' he repeated, 'and Our Lady of Lourdes.'

* * *

In the hotel I had my meals on a balcony that faced out over the sea. There was a breeze in the early morning. By midday the heat was unbearable, and Hubert, the waiter, would pull back my table under the awning. In the evening I would watch a fiery sun drop below a lurid, metallic sea. Then night would fall, and the surf became a curling phosphorescent line reaching on and on in the blue darkness.

Below the balcony there was a dance club with a canvas roof that was usually drawn back, so that the dancers and entertainers were visible. A sturdy, full-chested woman with a set smile used to hold her audience enthralled as she sang wild, nerve-throbbing songs that brought to my mind cow-boys and thudding hooves. I remarked on this to Hubert. 'It's music inspired by Israel's conquest of the Negev,' he explained as he leant over the balcony, a melancholy expression on his sensitive face. You cannot tell in Israel who your waiter, or your taxi-driver, will turn out to be. Perhaps an intellectual who has survived a Nazi concentration camp. Hubert was one of these. When he rolled up his sleeve his camp number was visible, tattooed on his forearm. He was a lonely creature with a passion for the music of Beethoven. I asked him if he was happy in Israel. 'I have everything I want,' he said, 'I am indebted to Israel for my life. And yet I am restless.' And he quoted Abraham Shlonsky:

> '*We burn to wander, wander, wander,*
> *Your command is stay.*
> *And we resent. And we conspire.*'

I remember Hubert for his courteous ways: and how, at the end of dinner, he used to put a multi-coloured ice-cream in front of me, though it did not appear on the menu.

CHAPTER VI

Jaffa

TEL AVIV is an extension of Jaffa. And Jaffa, Pliny says, was founded forty years after the Flood. Jewish tradition derives its name from Japhet, son of Noah. The Greeks, however, said it was called after Joppa, daughter of King Aeolus, who kept the winds imprisoned in a cave. In the harbour, black jagged rocks are pointed out as the place where the hero, Perseus, rescued Andromeda from the sea monster. The town is also associated with Saint George and the Dragon. Andromeda's monster, the dragon of Saint George, and the Philistine fish-god, Dagon, are probably one and the same, for Jaffa was a Phoenician colony in the land of the Philistines. Perhaps there should be added the whale that swallowed Jonah, for it was from Jaffa that Jonah set out on his voyage to Tarshish.

In the Middle Ages the pilgrims landed here. They were kept on board the galleys outside Andromeda's rocks while arrangements were made with the Moslems for their journey to Jerusalem. They used to see sharks and dolphins and turtles and other strange fish. Felix Faber, the Dominican, who kept a diary of his travels in the fifteenth century, mentions a large round fish 'like a winnowing fan', as well as others that had heads like dogs and long, drooping ears. At night, buffaloes used to come down to the shore and stand there in the sea – more than a hundred at once – with the water up to their necks.

A small mosque above the harbour marks the place of

Simon the Tanner's house, where Saint Peter, while waiting on the roof for a meal to be prepared, saw the vision of the living creatures let down from heaven in a sheet.

I approached it by a narrow lane, then an archway where an Arab was sitting on a rush stool. He wore a long, straight garment, much the shape of a Greek *chlamys*, made of a brown and white striped cotton, and on his head what is called a *keffiyeh*. The latter is a square of cloth, usually white, folded into a triangle and kept in place by two black strings made of camel-hair.

Beyond the arch there was a little courtyard with a fig tree in it, and a dog in a kennel. The dog barked, tugging at its chain. Then another Arab appeared and went ahead of me, up an outside staircase on to a roof that was flat except for two bulges caused by the domed ceiling of the mosque below. Close by was a minaret, and beyond it a white, candle-shaped lighthouse. Below, the waves broke upon the rocks of Andromeda.

A few minutes away, high above the sea, is the Franciscan church of Saint Peter. It is a large, pinky-yellow structure built in the seventeen hundreds on the foundation of the medieval citadel. There is nothing striking about it, other than the fact that it is there at all, dominating the landscape, in honour of a temperamental fisherman who betrayed his master.

I was in the church only once. It was not a feast day, yet the building was a blaze of light. If not in Saint Peter's honour, then in whose? Candles flickered on the altar and above it there was an illuminated cross and a dove encircled in light; more candles burnt in front of statues. The bright, warm atmosphere of the church contrasted with the desolation outside. Jaffa is a town that has suffered much. Formerly, the population was mainly Arab. The fighting has left debris and dust, rubble and skeleton houses. Yet enough of the old town remains to show what once it must have been. There are shabby fountains, open-fronted shops under ancient archways, a great white mosque supported by columns from Caesarea and Ashkelon. Asses and flocks of goats make the narrow streets impassable.

CHAPTER VII

The Dead Sea

'I GUESS the sun's going to make my eyes prick,' said the American woman, settling her dark glasses and giving a jab to her brimless hat. It was a pretty hat, made of violet-coloured velvet and decorated with beads; but hardly suitable for an expedition to the Dead Sea.

There were five of us. The American woman. Her middle-aged husband, who wore rimless spectacles and suffered from stomach ulcers. A tall young journalist – also American – with a baby face. The red-haired driver of the car, and myself.

The road from Tel Aviv to Beersheba ran at first through a well-watered area of banana and citrus groves with every now and then settlements of little pink-roofed houses enclosed by cypress hedges. Gradually the scene became less cultivated. We were out on an open rolling plain. To the east I saw another pink-roofed settlement and in the same glance, among palms and bananas, the devastated mud walls of what had been an Arab village. Away to the west were the hills of Judah; tawny-red, and dappled with outcrops of silvery limestone. The clouds flung great shadows on them. For though no rain falls in summer, clouds form, sometimes hiding the whole sky, as though a storm must surely break.

Here and there a *tel* marked the site of an ancient civilization. A signpost pointed the way to Gath. It was the country of David and the Philistines.

We passed the fortress-like home of Sheikh Suleiman, chief

of the only Bedouin tribe in Israel that has kept its identity. Then Bedouin encampments and asses and camels. Some of the camels stood etched against the sky, others merged into the landscape: for the wilder landscape of Israel is much the colour of a camel's hide.

The further we went the more barren the country. And now the moist heat of Tel Aviv had given place to a dry, scorching heat that was easier to bear. Here and there the flat, straight road was planted with eucalyptus trees, their cool, shifting shadows making a pattern on the sandy surface. The driver gave four reasons for planting the eucalyptus tree, which is not native to Israel.

First, there is the joy of planting a tree.

Secondly, a eucalyptus tree will grow anywhere, whether a desert or a swamp.

Thirdly, its pleasant foliage is a rest to eyes that are tired from glare, dust, and sunlight.

Finally, in time of war these trees are a camouflage for army traffic, and so a protection against attack from the air.

At Beersheba we went into a restaurant where we had fried eggs with salad and glasses of lemon-flavoured tea. It was a simple place, but roomy and clean, with white cloths on the tables, and in one corner a basin with a towel hanging from the wall. The American woman went across to wash her hands, looked at the towel, said 'Gawd' and came back to her seat. Through the window I could see little pepper trees lining the streets. A donkey brayed.

When we went out, Sheikh Suleiman was sitting in front of the café, resplendent in blue trimmed with red and silver, and with him two younger men, hardly less splendid. Some tourists stood staring. The American journalist whipped out a camera and edged his way to the front.

In the hills about Beersheba, Abraham led his flocks to

pasture. Here he made a covenant with Abimelech, and dug a well. Isaac, too, lived here and built an altar and called upon the name of the Lord. . . . Beersheba used to be the southernmost point of Israel, and it still has the character of a frontier town. I felt as if I had come to the end of civilization.

* * *

As we got into the car, the driver was handed a rifle and cartridges. 'Security regulations,' he said, 'in case of Arab infiltrations'. He flung the cartridges on to the seat beside him, then settled the rifle with its barrel pointing towards the back of the car.

'This'll make a write-up,' said the journalist. The American woman gave me a dig in the back. 'We're for it,' she said.

The heat became yet more intense. I could not bear my hand on the metal of the window frame. The scenery, too, was wilder than anything that we had seen, and on an immense scale. There were mountains, some altogether bare, others covered with a low-growing scrub or strewn with boulders. And above, a burning, merciless sky. In this wilderness, Hagar, the bondwoman, had wandered with her son, Ishmael. We went on and on. The black tarmac road stretched ahead between bleached, desolate mountains. 'I shan't be sorry to see Tel Aviv,' said the American woman leaning over to me and giving her hat a tug. She had almost to shout because the radio was blaring a wild Israeli tune. Its throbbing rhythm was as monotonous as the mountains that reached on without end.

A lorry rattled past coming from the potash works at Sodom. Then we were held up by a camel that had planted itself across the road. It was some moments before the animal moved, turning its head as it did so, and looking at us superciliously. Another time, when we slowed down, Bedouin women, dressed in black, gathered about the car. Coins hung upon their foreheads. Their faces were tattooed, and their finger nails stained with henna. There were little boys, too, who smiled at us, showing white teeth with gold fillings.

I had lost count of time when the road began to drop. Down. Down. The heat, fiercer than ever, came in waves through the window. Suddenly, below, was the Dead Sea and the dead world that lies about it.

A mist hung upon jade, blue-shadowed water, making the mountains on the further side look like a cloud of lavender suspended in the sky. To the south, the green of the water merged into a leprous white that might have been a scar on the earth's surface. On closer view the more vivid white took the shape of salt-pans: the rest was a desert of naked marl hills, flat-topped, fantastic in shape and pale as death. It was Sodom and Gomorrah.

The road dropped to the level of the water, then ran north keeping, roughly, to the line of the sea. On the inland side rocks towered, jagged and devoid of colour.

A vulture wheeled above us, a big white bird with black on the wings. This is the Egyptian vulture, a great scavenger, but also a coward. Even a rat fills it with terror. Colonel Meinertzhagen in his *Birds of Arabia* tells how he offered one of these birds a sausage on a string; at the slightest pull on the string it took flight. The Egyptian vulture will bathe in only a few inches of water, then, when wet all over, sit on a rock to dry.

We passed the potash works, its great shafts and girders seeming only to add to the desolation. Boats lay upon the sea: there were perhaps a dozen, but not a man on board. A dead fleet I thought. And so it was. Before the fighting these boats had been used to take potash to a factory on the north shore which is now in Jordan.

Soon the road became no more than a track, strewn with stones. It took us to an immense cliff of silver-pale salt rock – the pillar of salt into which Lot's wife was changed. Behind it, reached back the caves of the mountain called Jebel Usdum. We went into their darkness guided by wild-looking men, stripped to the waist and carrying torches that were made from iron stakes supporting tins of sand drenched in kerosene. The men with their sun-scorched torsos and sizzling flaring brands, looked like medieval torturers. They went ahead, disappearing and appearing, through twisting passages, up and down, into caverns, among huge salt blocks and pale stalactites. I have never liked caves. These filled me with terror. They brought back childhood nightmares about Lot's wife and Sodom and Gomorrah.

We drank mineral waters beneath a shelter open on four sides, with under it a trestle table and benches. It looked paltry, in some way absurd, in this place of desolation.

I sat under the shadow of a rock, a few yards from the sea. The water spread before me was a sparkling blue, with reaching out at its further side the shining white peninsula called the Tongue. Beyond the Tongue there were mountains. In this sea, I reflected, no living creature could survive. Nor did it seem strange that this should be so: for, despite the colour and the sunlight, the atmosphere was sinister and oppressive, as of a place accursed. Small wonder that, as of the Vergilian lake Avernus, there had grown up the myth that no bird could fly across its waters.

> *'Quam super haud ullae poterant inpune volantes*
> *Tendere iter pinnis.'*

I walked down to where the waves broke sluggishly on a gravel beach strewn with driftwood stripped of its bark. I dipped my hand into the water. When I took it out, it had an oily feeling. Then, as it dried, tiny crystals formed on the skin and I felt a pricking sensation – that was what Brother Felix must have meant when he said it was as if his hands were 'full of fleas and gnats'.

* * *

On the way back to Beersheba a tyre burst. As we waited by the roadside, I watched the wheatears flitting from boulder to boulder, calling to one another. Unlike the English bird of that name, they were black and white. The ground between the boulders was covered with a low-growing sweet-smelling herb. There was the scrub, too, which is called *spina christi*, a thorn with savage spines. Suddenly on the spur of the hill, a Bedouin came into view, mounted on a horse and carrying a rifle slung over his shoulder. The sight of him troubled the American woman. 'I guess today's been long enough,' she said, giving a tug to the violet hat.

The sun hung low in the sky when we stopped at Beersheba. The café was crowded with Arabs, and the floor strewn with the litter of the day. The driver sat with his elbows on the table, eating interminably, as it seemed to us. The rest of us had enormous slices of water melon and tea with lemon. As we were getting into the car a dark wild-haired child jumped in ahead and settled herself in my seat. She was holding a tin lid covered with pieces of sticky nut toffee. 'Sweetmeat! Buy sweetmeat!' she cried shrilly. We took some, and she jumped out bowing and shouting, '*Merci, Madame. Merci, Monsieur. Shalom! Shalom!*' She was a Moroccan immigrant.

It was after nine o'clock when we drove into Tel Aviv: we had left before eight that morning. Pavements were crowded and cafés a dazzle of light. . . . There were two windows in my room. One looked across to a room opposite with its curtains still undrawn. Two young men were sitting on a bed playing dominoes and talking in loud voices. Highly coloured drinks stood on a table near by. Through the other window music came up from the dance club. Looking down, I could see the woman with the set smile, her plump arm raised, her audience staring at her, enthralled. I had come back from one wilderness to another.

* * *

As I finished dinner Dr Z. came over to my table. He was a Polish Jew with a shock of stiff grey hair and an intelligent tormented face. The music throbbed, then it would cease and the night be filled with the murmur of the sea. We talked about Sodom, then the Old Testament and the prophets. Then about religion in general, each feeling for our words, for fear of giving offence to the other.

'I respect Catholicism,' he said. 'It has tradition, discipline, dignity, ceremonial. Your Mass has the quality of a Greek drama. . . . But had you been brought up an Orthodox Jew you would not have become a Catholic.

'You would have found all this in the Jewish religion. As it is, you were starved.'

'I, too, respect Jewish Orthodoxy,' I said. 'But Catholicism is its culmination, the fulfilment of the prophets.'

He smiled indulgently, and shook his head.

Then I asked him a question that was much in my mind. 'What,' I said, 'is your fundamental objection to Christianity?'

He thought for a moment.

'Not, as you may think, the Christian persecution of the Jews – that is beside the point. And I won't tell you, as many a Jew will, that the romantic countryside of Galilee is a breeding-ground for dreamers and would-be Messiahs. After all your Ireland is no less romantic.

'No, the fundamental objection is the Incarnation, as you call it. To the ancient Greek mind with its anthropomorphic conception of religion it was conceivable. To a Jew, never. Belief in a Messiah, a leader sent by God, yes. . . . But God in human form, the Second Person of the Trinity – it's blasphemous. The law of Moses forbade us make an image of God in stone. You make it in flesh.'

I pursued the matter no further. For what point to argue the Incarnation with someone who, on *a priore* grounds, has already dismissed it as impossible. But I did say: 'Yet there are Jews who have become Christians?'

'Yes, for material gain.'

'But what of Père X?' I went on, naming a priest familiar to us both.

'Père X?' he murmured thoughtfully. 'Some people, Christians as well as Jews, call him a mountebank, others a saint.'

'And you?'

'I keep an open mind. . . . And yet a Jew who becomes a Christian and is still loved, as Père X. is, by his own people, must have in him something of the saint.'

CHAPTER VIII

Elath

'*And King Solomon made a navy of ships in Ezion-Geber which is beside Eloth on the shore of the Red Sea in the land of Edom.*' KINGS

THE AEROPLANE dipped down, and the sea and mountains rushed up to meet it. The sea shone like a great Burma sapphire: the mountains were the dusky purple-red of crushed rose petals.

Modern Elath is the southernmost point of Israel; a desert outpost at the tip of the Red Sea's eastern gulf.

But it will soon be more than an outpost. So said the bronzed young giant with the hair and eyes of a Viking, as he pointed to what had already been achieved. There were houses and an hotel, a school and a café, a spear-fishing club, and a store such as you might see in a Middle West town. Saplings had been planted and there were cacti with pointed, sword-blade leaves, and a few, struggling flowers. A cultural centre was being built out of the same purple-red stone as the mountains. A windmill working a generator purred in the hot breeze.

'Elath will be a fashionable resort,' the young man went on, 'as big as Tel Aviv. . . . Israel's Riviera. A port, too, as important as Haifa. . . . From here will be exported ore and minerals, phosphates and potash. . . . Elath is Israel's back window opening on to the east.'

I listened and I looked, but in a dazed kind of way. The hot wind blew and the windmill purred. The sun was beating down, and the mountains had a strange, hypnotic effect on me. They stood all about, rising in great escarpments. The earth below them was scorched, and the sky a blinding blue. Surely, there had never been a time without the mountains. They were there before the ancient biblical Elath was built on the further side of the gulf, where Aqaba now stands; and when this new Elath would have crumbled to dust they would still be there.

We went into a wooden building where a dark-skinned girl in a petunia-coloured dress was weaving a crimson and blue carpet. 'An immigrant from India,' the Viking said. Then to the little maritime museum, pleasantly arranged, with photographs of under-water fishing and a display of strange sea creatures. There were cat-faced shark and Patagonian lobsters, bird fish and butterfly fish, sea urchins and filigree starfish – the star of Solomon that has five points and King David's six-pointed star.

We came out into the glaring sunlight. The Viking was talking about a factory for making paper out of a plant called *yunkus* that grows in the Wadi Arava. The rose-red mountains quivered in the heat haze. I felt that I had seen these mountains before. Pitiless mountains under a pitiless sky. Mexico kept coming into my mind.

We got into a small bus. The professor from Tennessee, his wife, the Viking and myself. The professor had a quiet face: he looked like the rector of a country parish in England. His wife reminded me of one of my Edwardian aunts; she wore a lavender voile dress high at the neck and trimmed with black velvet bows. Her watch was attached to a gold chain that hung round her neck. At first she had seemed to me a little stern. Then she leant across and laid her hand on my arm, her oyster-coloured glove wrinkling about her wrist. 'I noticed you in the aeroplane,' she said. 'You're adventurous to come alone.' There was an Irish intonation in her voice.

She and her husband were Jewish. They had come from the States to see the new Israel. She was troubled at some of the things she had seen – at the decline of Orthodox religion, the emphasis on material progress, the tendency in the *kibbutzim* to bring up children apart from their parents. She sighed: 'We're old fashioned, I suppose.'

'What does your husband think?' I asked.

'He too is troubled. But he says we must have patience.'

'Yes,' he said, 'we must have patience. God will not forsake the children of Israel.'

The bus rattled along in clouds of dust, bumping over stones, almost flinging us off our seats. The Viking was driving. Every other moment his head turned round, as he told us about this or that. Above us the range of Sinai rose vast and desolate, its only vegetation a few scattered thorn trees. 'It was down that wadi that Moses led the children of Israel,' the Viking was saying. . . .

We got out to look at a granite quarry. The ground was strewn with fragments of black stone that sparkled with minute specks of silver. The professor picked up some pieces and put them into the pocket of his alpaca coat. There was a little tree – some kind of thorn with tiny yellow balls hanging from it. I asked the Viking its name. He did not know. Besides, he was talking about plans for manufacturing salt out of seawater by means of evaporation.

We were near the frontier of Egypt. Across the gulf the coast of Saudi Arabia stretched away. To the north, at the water's edge, I saw the white houses of Aqaba which is in Jordan. T. E. Lawrence had a base at Aqaba, and the Crusaders built a castle there. Beyond, were the mountains of Edom, streaked with brimstone. . . . Four countries met. Saudi Arabia and Jordan, Israel and Egypt. The sea washing their shores was the same that broke upon the beaches of India and Mozambique.

The mountains were grim and old as time. The sea was young, as on the day of Creation: its little dancing waves rustled, then broke in foam on the shell-strewn shore. And yet on these waters the ships of Tarshish had sailed, and the ships of Nineveh. . . . It is a fairy sea. Anemones sway in its crystalline depths. Its corals are rose-pink and crimson; madder, ivory and green. Striped and spangled fish dart among their branches.

* * *

I stood at the airport with the professor and his wife, and a group of young Israeli soldiers on their way back to Lydda. Little boys hovered about us, trying to sell bottles of coloured sand arranged in intricate patterns. The heat throbbed. The windmill hummed. The Viking was talking about the pipe-line laid through the Negev. . . . He shook us by the hand. '*Shalom! Shalom!*'

From the aeroplane I watched the sea and mountains slip away. We flew north, passing over other mountains, tawny as the skin of a lion and patterned with pale markings like the bones of a fish.

CHAPTER IX

Ashkelon

THE HEAT was violent, but it was dry and tempered by a breeze blowing in from the sea. The leaves of the little poplars made a pattering sound.

Ashkelon Afridar is a garden city built above the dunes and a great sweep of strand. South African Jews provided the money for it, and were responsible for its planning – and it is planned to the smallest detail. Its civic centre, made of purple-red brick, is simple in design. An arcade protects shops and cafés from the sun. There are lawns, and flower-beds gay with geraniums, and smart blue kiosks patterned with white Hebrew lettering. The comfortable, sophisticated hotel takes its name from the god Dagon whose worship in these parts goes back almost to the beginning of time. The intelligently arranged museum displays finds from ancient Ashkelon and the surrounding country, and Roman marbles set around a lily pond are mirrored in its water.

There was an air of holiday making. Bare-legged women in beach-wear were sitting in the shadow of the arcade drinking orange juice through straws. At the next table were two boys with side-curls. They wore skull-caps – one white satin embroidered with blue flowers, the other green, with a yellow star. Sitting beside them was a Yemenite woman with her hair in plaits. She was wearing a thick, dark-blue garment heavily brocaded and boots that came up to her calves. A child with her was dressed in much the same way. They reminded me of Laplanders.

* * *

'Gaza shall be forsaken and Ashkelon a desolation.' JEREMIAH

A flat sandy road ran to ancient Ashkelon. At first it went past vineyards and olive groves and citrus plantations with now and again glimpses of sand-dunes and a sea that was brilliantly blue. Then the scene became desolate. There were tamarisks and ragged-looking palms and a quantity of sycamores. In the days of the Bible the sycamores of this region were famous. King David set Baal-hanan, the Gederite, to be in charge of them. They became a symbol of plenty, so that of Solomon it was said 'the king made silver to be in Jerusalem as stones, and cedar made he to be as the sycamore trees that are in the vale for abundance'.

The road had given place to a rough track. Scrub and stiff parched grasses reached shoulder-high. Tiny white-shelled snails clung in hundreds to the leafless cinnamon-coloured twigs of a low-growing shrub. A red-legged bird darted across my path and every now and then I would see a great brown and black crow perching on a branch.

Suddenly I saw the walls of ancient Ashkelon. On one side. Then on another. They stood up, from among trees and scrub, and then, again, were so overgrown as hardly to be visible. The atmosphere of the lonely ruined walls, the tangled growth and the silence, was oppressive and mysterious: in such a place many secrets of the past were surely hidden.

There was a hollow in the ground enclosed by a stone wall built into the earth and topped with barbed wire. In it were broken marbles. Huge drums of creamy stone or rose-flushed porphyry. Giant capitals carved with acanthus leaves, and reputed to be from Herod's Porch of the Hundred Pillars. A mother wearing the turreted crown of Isis, and, looking over her shoulder, a child. There were two winged figures, with shattered faces that had the blank appearance of masks: one carried a palm, the other stood poised above a globe supported on the shoulders of a bowed and struggling Atlas. These marbles were from Roman times, but Ashkelon goes back in history to the Canaanites and Phoenicians, the Philistines and Egyptians. Their dark past seemed to be there too, brooding over the ruins of Rome.

It was to this place that the eccentric Lady Hester Stanhope came in the early years of the last century, with her tents and her torchbearers, her watermen, couriers and mules. She came to find gold, but she left devastation. The ground is still littered with fragments of a statue of Hercules that in a fit of temperamental rage she smashed into a thousand pieces for no better reason than to salve her pride.

From the marbles a path led through a confusion of undergrowth to the cliff's edge. Great columns built horizontally into the sea wall – to give strength where the facing had fallen away – jutted out like the barrels of guns. Through a gaping hole in the turf I looked down into what once had been a reservoir to give water to ships. Here the ships of the Philistines had anchored, and those of King Herod and the Crusaders.

To the south the coast reached away to Gaza – the surf a white unbroken line. It is an inhospitable coast; at no place does the land draw back to give welcome to the sea.

* * *

The tomb was a little way inland. A mound by the roadside, with no habitation near. I went down the steps into its darkness. After the dazzling brightness of the sun it seemed at first to be no more that a black hole. Then the darkness faded, patterns and colours took shape. What I saw had a beauty that suggested an Italian primitive.

On the wall facing me two nymphs reclined, holding pitchers from which water flowed into a pool below. There were fish in the pool, and at its margin reeds and flowering plants in which marsh birds nested. A crane was fishing. An ox was entering the water to drink.

The vaulted roof was patterned with a trellised vine. Pictures filled the spaces between. Pan was playing his reed pipe. A naked boy on tip-toe reached his arms to pick a cluster of grapes, while another bent over a basket. A hound was setting upon a speckled gazelle. Birds offered food to a stag; others fluttered or perched among the vine leaves, or pecked at the grapes. A huge Gorgon's mask with snakes for hair stared down. But there was also the calm beautiful face of Demeter, goddess of the Eleusinian Mysteries.

The paintings were faded, and yet they had not lost their freshness. They conveyed joy and wonder, and also a deeper aesthetic quality: the splendour of life was there, but the fear of death, too, symbolized by the face of the Gorgon, and, as an anodyne to fear, the perception of things spiritual revealed through the Mysteries of Eleusis.

I came out into the world above. After the colours in the tomb the evening light seemed pallid and silvery: I wondered which was more real, the world about me, or the world of the painted tomb.

CHAPTER X

Caesarea

I

BETWEEN Tel Aviv and Haifa there was a turning to Caesarea. On the left was a *maarbarah* or transition camp – that is, a temporary home for newly arrived immigrants from which they are later moved. It looked derelict compared with the settlement of new, concrete houses on the opposite side. Then came a banana grove. A breeze stirred the big, indented leaves, making them flicker with shafts of silver. Beyond the banana grove was a great open space. Nothing but the sky above and the hot breeze blowing. Here, perhaps a couple of feet below the level of the ground, were the excavations.

Two statues of ancient Romans, both headless, were facing one another. That they had no heads did not matter. There they sat, silent and mysterious, looking across at each other. One was made of creamy marble. A toga fell over the left shoulder, leaving bare the muscular chest and abdomen. The left leg was bent, the right came forward, showing the foot in its sandal. The second figure was even more forceful. It was cut in a purple-red stone, dark as grapes, and the whole body was covered by the folds of the toga. The sombre colouring and the shrouded figure created an atmosphere of secrecy and muffling silence, and so heightened the air of mystery. To the right of the purple figure, and reaching across to the one opposite, ran a low wall with two pillars embedded in it. One of the pillars was smashed, its upper half resting on the top of the wall. All the broken splendour of Imperial Rome was in those silent figures seated there among the stones and shattered pillars, while overhead the sun shone, and the breeze shivered in the banana leaves.

A few yards from the figures there was digging going on. A gang of men with pickaxes and shovels was clearing away the earth, which was heaped into rubber bags, made from motor tyres, then handed along a chain of helpers, and tipped into a lorry. They were swarthy, bearded men, wearing bright-coloured shirts and high-crowned straw hats with enormous brims. They looked for all the world like pirates. Supervising them, was a sun-tanned young woman in blue shorts, with a cigarette in her mouth. She gave orders in a peremptory ringing voice.

'She's got them in hand,' Isaac said to me.

Isaac was a handsome young man with dark, sparkling eyes – yet not so young as he looked. He had come to Israel from Germany with his parents and sister in the early days of Hitler's persecution. Having served first in the British Army he was afterwards an officer in the Jewish Army of Liberation. When he heard that I was going on to Jordan he asked me to enquire of Glubb Pasha how it was that the Arabs, trained and disciplined by British officers, had not beaten the Israelis who, in comparison, were untrained and few in number.

'But I can tell you the answer myself,' he went on. 'We were fighting for our homes, in desperation, knowing that we had no retreat – like the Greeks at Marathon. Again, because, like the Greeks, we belonged to a democratic state, we were able, each of us, to act on our own, to use our intelligence. The "Other Side" were dependent on their officers. We used to say: "Kill their officers, and we've won!" '

He talked of the siege of Jerusalem, how, for weeks,

the defenders had lived on bread and water. The night of the truce, Isaac and some of his companions reached Tel Aviv. 'When we jumped out of the lorry,' he said, 'the people on the pavement shrank from us. We were unshaven and our uniforms blood-stained and in rags. I'd half a dozen Arab knives stuck in my belt. . . . I went home and had a shower – one, then another. Oh, the joy of the water streaming over me! Then I ate ice-cream and was sick!'

From the excavations we went on in the direction of the sea, past tamarisks and then fig trees. A man was shaking down the fruit with a long pole: the scene reminded me of a painting on a Greek vase. Presently Isaac got out of the car and came back with his hands full of figs: they were pink inside and very sweet.

We sat on high ground above the harbour, close to some Herodian earthworks and the remains of a Crusader fort. Isaac was still talking about the war.

'Did you notice a rusted jeep on the road outside Jerusalem?' he asked me.

I remembered it: it was near Abu Ghosh, where an Arab village rests against the hill and a Crusader church is built above an ancient reservoir of cool, clear water. 'That jeep was mine,' Isaac went on, 'Arabs ambushed us, when we were trying to get supplies through to Jerusalem. I was the only one in it who escaped alive.'

In Israel there are many reminders of the fighting. A battered car, left there by the roadside for all to see. A jeep overturned. A bombed building repaired only in part. 'Honourable Scars,' Isaac called them. They were left, too, he explained, as a warning—that none might forget.

I tried to collect my thoughts on Caesarea. In Roman times it had been the seat of the Governor. Here Saint Paul appeared before Felix and then Festus. It was while he was in prison at Caesarea that Agrippa and his Queen Berenice had come with great pomp to see him. Paul spoke at length, until Festus, in exasperation, interrupted in a loud voice telling him that too much learning had turned his wits. Agrippa, however, was impressed. 'Thou almost persuadest me to become a Christian,' he said.

For those who are not antiquarians ruins can be stark and formidable, or merely dull. But at Caesarea they were softened by waving tamarisks and the shining green of fig trees. Below, was the sea; sapphire in the distance, and near at hand a clear green, like liquid glass. It swept landward, its currents crossing upon themselves, then pouring over the battered jetty and licking the columns that strewed the beach.

II

As we went south from Caesarea, Isaac stopped the car to give a lift to a Yemenite.

He was an old man slight of build, with a delicately beautiful face. The skin was deeply furrowed, the eyes dark and solemn. It was a face full of dignity and patience. When he spoke, it lit up and the eyes shone. A lorry overtook us, giving out a whiff of dried fish. He made a grimace and gesticulated with his small, finely shaped hands. His bare feet were also small and white with dust. He had with him a rubber bag stuffed with greenery. Lemon leaves, he explained, that he was bringing from a cousin he had visited. They were for his hens; to give the eggs a pleasant flavour. He was bringing them especially, because in the settlement to which he belonged he could not pick the lemon leaves. They belonged to all in common. It would not do if one person were to strip the trees. Others would do the same.

What then? All this was said in Hebrew, and interpreted to me by Isaac.

We stopped for a few minutes at the settlement. Other Yemenites, much like himself, gathered round the old man, questioning him, and welcoming him. The place was like an eastern village. A man was sitting on the ground outside a wooden hut, weighing vegetables on scales. Under a bamboo-covered shelter women waited while the carcass of a sheep was being cut up; flies crawled on the raw, red flesh, and the hide hung from the roof. A little girl was selling prickly-pears. A cobbler sat at his bench nailing a strip of embroidery across the front of a shoe. There were scraggy white hens picking up what they could.

The Yemenites are a strange and wonderful people.

They moved in their thousands, carrying their prayer books and scrolls, their pots and pans, wandering over mountain and desert, from their home in Saudi Arabia to Hashed, near Aden, from where aeroplanes transported them to Israel. It was a mass migration, like the wanderings of the Israelites. Thousands died on the way, of sickness and hunger, heat and cold. Even so, those who reached the Promised Land were as many as fifty thousand, and the aeroplanes that took them made more than four hundred flights. This was in the summer of 1950. The dramatic story is told by Sholom Barer in his book *The Magic Carpet*. Perhaps a poet will someday tell it, for it is an epic theme.

By western standards the Yemenites may seem primitive. They know nothing of machinery or plumbing, use amulets and wrap their babies in black cloths tied with string. They are, however, skilled silversmiths and makers of beautiful jewellery and embroidery which are displayed in the shops and hotels in Jerusalem and Tel Aviv.

Moreover, they are a people with an exalted spiritual

vision which shows itself in an implicit faith in God and in the coming of the Messiah. It is said of them that they alone of the Oriental immigrants have not only brought their religion with them to Israel, but have remained true to it in the face of contrary influences. They have, too, a deep regard for learning. Much of the money they earn is put away for the education of their numerous children. Sometimes their earnings are considerable, as unlike, for example, the Iraqis – many of whom before coming to Israel were no more than beggars or perhaps newspaper sellers – the Yemenites know how to work for the reason that they were able to survive in Arabia only through their own efforts. They differ, again, from other Orientals in their attitude towards women whom they hold in great regard, consulting them in all matters of consequence. On festive occasions the women wear beautifully embroidered tunics and bonnets that are decorated with coins.

The stories about the Yemenites are many. Some say they are one of the lost tribes, others that they travelled from Jerusalem to the Yemen in the train of the Queen of Sheba when she went back to her kingdom after visiting King Solomon. Others say that they left Jerusalem after the destruction of the first Temple, in response to the warning of Jeremiah that those who stayed would perish, and those who left be spared. Later, when Cyrus, King of Persia, liberated the Jews from their captivity in Babylon, Ezra, the prophet, bade all the children of Israel return to the Holy City. . . . The Yemenites, however, refused, arguing that God had given them a Holy Land of their own. The prophet cursed them for their disobedience, and to this curse they attribute the misfortunes that later afflicted them. For though Mahommed himself is said to have given them a letter of protection and they lived for long periods on friendly terms with the Moslems, yet their sufferings were great indeed. By day they worked as smiths and potters, weavers and armourers, engravers and minters, but at night they returned to the isolation of the ghetto, living in great contempt and subject to all manner of restrictions whereby they might not build a house higher than a Moslem, be found sitting in the presence of a Moslem, raise their voice in prayer, mourn their dead or blow the ram's horn loudly.

* * *

We came to Ramle in the mid-day heat. It is an Arab town with white domed buildings and a great white tower. The muezzin was giving the call to prayer. I could see him on the balcony of the minaret: he wore a *tarbush* swathed in white. We waited for him to come down, as Isaac was anxious he should take us to the Great Mosque which was a few minutes away.

We walked through narrow streets, under archways. I imagined that the Old City of Jerusalem would be something like this. There were high walls and glimpses of courtyards with trees and shrubs in them. A woman passed, her face totally veiled in black. Others wore veils that covered only the lower part of the face. Men sat in open-fronted cafés playing cards and drinking coffee, or smoking *narghiles* with sleepy, half-closed eyes.

The Great Mosque was once a Crusader church. It was a big, strong building with pillars dividing it into three naves. It looked shabby for it had been washed with white, then left to fall into disrepair. Even so, it was beautiful, and dignified, and very cool. In an open doorway an Arab lay asleep under a blue quilted cover, with on the floor beside him a pile of water melons arranged in a pyramid.

From the mosque, we went to the monastery of Saint

Joseph of Arimathea, which was used by Napoleon as a staff-headquarters. The door stood open. Isaac went to look for one of the fathers, while I waited in a parlour. I could hear a man's voice, querulous, and loud, as though he were speaking to someone who was deaf. Presently Isaac came back with a calm-faced woman – she was a monastery cook, he told me. She took us into the church, then into a chapel where there was a figure of the dead Christ with the blood of his wounds upon him. It was then I heard the loud querulous voice for the second time. It was behind me. I looked round, and saw a wizened face contorted with hate. 'Look,' he said, pointing to the wounded Christ. 'The Jews did that.' There was silence, then I heard another voice: 'Not the Jews, all of us.' It came from a young man wearing the habit of a Benedictine. I had not noticed him till then, standing there in the shadows.

CHAPTER XI

Nazareth

THE ROAD dipped down and the camels were coming up. One. Then another. Then another. They had red tassels on their heads, and they were laden with sacks so enormous that they seemed to take up the width of the road. They were coming up from Nazareth. . . .

'Can any good thing come out of Nazareth?' Nathaniel asked. It seemed to be no different now. In Jerusalem, in Tel Aviv: 'Nazareth?' they said. 'There's not much there. You'll see it in half a day, a day perhaps. A shabby place, behind the times, riddled with Communism. You won't want to stay there.'

It lay below me, the town despised of men, but chosen by God before the creation of the world; square stone houses, towers and belfries, red roofs and cypress trees – closed about by the hills, like a rose protected by its leaves.

* * *

Women were coming away from the Well of Mary. They carried pitchers or cans on their heads, their bright-coloured veils hung low over their black dresses, and their feet were bare. Then, I came to a wide straggling street. Little boys with dark tousled hair or heads closely shaven went up and down on donkeys. Most of the men wore the long striped tunic, with either a *keffiyeh* or a crochetted skull-cap. Some were in European clothes and bareheaded. One had a cossack hat made of astrakhan.

Along the street there was a restaurant called the English Bar. Not that there was anything particularly English about it, except two paintings: one, naked trees above snow; the other, swans on a lake against a background of flaming autumn leaves. I liked the English Bar with its cool, flagged floor, thick pink-washed walls and vaulted ceiling. You could have a simple, well-cooked meal – or, perhaps, a salad, called *humous*, made from chickpeas and olive oil with garlic, *simsim*, parsley and a flavour of lemon, and with it flat circles of bread of a double thickness. . . . I liked the young Arab owner, Peter Abu Nasser. He would be there first thing in the morning – a smile on his face, his spotless nylon shirt hanging loose over his trousers, rings on his fingers and round his neck a chain with a gold cross. It was pleasant, too, to wile away the heat of the day chatting to him, and sipping Turkish coffee or cognac or arak, while out in the street the sun beat down and the hooves of donkeys pattered.

In the English Bar I became conscious, for the first time, of the Arab language. Peter talked it to his friends – though Hebrew and English and French were also spoken round me – and, sometimes, in the morning a reading of the Koran would come across on the radio. Arabic has an elusive, unsubstantial quality which contrasts with the solidity that characterizes Hebrew. This comes out, too, in the lettering of the two languages. Hebrew is made up of thick strokes, Arabic twists and twirls as though it belonged to a world of fantasy.

* * *

Nazareth is a jumble of a town. Off the main street there are lanes and alleys and flights of steps that, if you know which to follow, will take you to the market with its cobblers and

A Roman statue at Caesarea

The Victory at Ashkelon

Arab refugee camp: supplementary rations for the children

carpenters, its Turkish open-fronted shops, its booths that sell prickly-pears, and peppers and figs; yokes and harness; rope and baskets; pots and pans and pitchers; lace; rosaries; strings of Moslem prayer-beads and camels carved out of olive wood. There are churches everywhere, many of them shabby homely buildings with little that is artistic to commend them.

A door in a wall opens into a courtyard in front of the Mensa Christi church with in it a great block of limestone on which they tell you Christ fed his disciples. The Greek Catholic church adjoins a chapel built on the site of the synagogue in which Christ preached. The dim, candle-lit church of the Orthodox Greeks is over the spring that feeds Mary's Well. The church of Saint Joseph stands above what is said to have been his workshop. The church of the Annunciation is being rebuilt, so that to approach the cave where the Angel appeared, you must walk a rickety plank with below, on either side, gaping cisterns and great holes where the earth has been excavated.

Close to the church of the Annunciation are the Terra Sancta buildings in which the Franciscans have their school. A stone staircase leads up to an office where Brother Roberts sits at his desk, a cigar in his mouth, papers cluttered about him. He is a burly American with a loud laugh and a word for everyone. The telephones ring. The door opens and shuts. There is a continual coming and going: an Arab teacher belonging to the school; then a Jewish official from Haifa; then a pilgrim in need of hospitality. The high-ceilinged room has character. In one corner there is an aquarium, in another an old-fashioned black stove. A Scouts' banner rests against a wall hung with a painting of Saint Louis, and a stone carved with the crossed hands that are the Franciscan coat of arms. A bookcase contains works on psychology and education, writings on the Holy Land and the plays of Shakespeare.

* * *

Nazareth is an Arab town, but the Arabs in Israel are a minority. For 'security reasons' restrictions are put on their movements. They must have a permit to go here, to go there. A permit for Haifa, a permit for Hule, a permit for Safed, and so on. That is why they stand about in the courtyard or on the steps of the police headquarters; or they sit on a bench inside with papers in their hands, and on their faces the expression of boredom that you see on the faces of out-patients in a hospital queue. The Police Superintendent is a stocky Jew with shrewd black eyes in a furrowed face. His office, too, is a place of comings and goings. A policeman in khaki salutes, delivers a message, salutes again and is gone. A blonde-headed woman who looks like a Scandinavian but is an Arab resident of Nazareth, has a request to make. A Greek priest comes in, bows, murmurs something that is scarcely audible and sits down. Coffee is brought in tiny cups without handles. It is offered first to the priest, who takes it and passes it on to me. The Superintendent is anxious to please: one of his men, he says, will show me the town: a jeep will be available. He refers to me in conversation as 'the Lady Hamilton!'

* * *

Betharam. I first heard the word in the English Bar, tossed to and fro between Peter Abu Nasser and a Jewish friend who had driven me to Nazareth from Haifa. Then I heard it between the same Jewish friend and Brother Roberts; and then, again, at the police headquarters. The syllables had a ring of unreality, like 'Abracadabra' or 'Open Sesame'. I knew that the word was being used in relation to myself, but as the conversations were in either Arabic or Hebrew, I could not tell its significance. Then it was explained to me. Betharam was the name of a hospice for pilgrims run by French Fathers – a place at which I could stay.

If the word seemed hardly real, this was no less true of the hospice. There were no pilgrims, no visitors. It was as though I were alone in the great cool building with its stone stairways and corridors that were tiled with pearl-white marble and lit with windows looking out on to pines and cypresses and, in the distance, a sweep of pale, red earth broken by silver outcrops of limestone. The heat of the day was sweet with the scent of the pines and loud with the grating of cicadas: and over a wall I would see a huge camel sitting on the white dusty road and Arabs squatting near by talking lazily.

In a week I met no one at the hospice except the 'Little Father' – for so I came to think of him – with his frail sallow face and on his head something that was nearer a pill-box than a biretta. He would slip past me on the stairs with a smile and a murmured greeting in French. Or he would be winding the grandfather clock that seemed incongruous standing in the corridor beside a window through which I could see Mount Tabor. When I came in at night he was there, waiting to lock up. He would go in front of me switching on the lights in the passages, the sash of his soutane swaying as he moved – he looked for all the world like a little bat. Then, bowing me on my way, he would leave me with a murmured '*Bon soir, mademoiselle, dormez bien*'. I used to hear the flitter of his feet growing fainter, and the grinding of bolts. . . . Up in my room, I would go out on to the balcony and watch the tufted pines black and motionless against the sky, and huge silver stars so close, it would seem, to the earth that it was as if I had only to reach out my hand to touch them. And I would say: 'They will never believe me in England if I tell them how big and how bright are the stars that look down upon Nazareth.'

* * *

At night you could feel the stillness of Nazareth. Footsteps echoed and figures slipped by in the darkness. Once, when the moon was up, I saw a woman standing by the Well of Mary her hand raised to the pitcher on her head, and at her side a child.

But it was not always stillness.

One night there was a wedding, with music and dancing, rifle shots and the flare of torches. . . . And, on the Eve of the Assumption, a party on the roof of Peter Abu Nasser's house. We had cognac and nuts, goat's cheese, sweet biscuits, melon and grapes. On the hill above, the Salesian College was flood-lit and the town below a blaze of light. Lights shone on roofs, in doors, in windows. The cross on the Greek church was picked out in light. Music blared from loud-speakers. Rockets shot to the stars, then fell in showers of gold.

'Are people any different, any better for being born and bred in Nazareth? Are they more fervent Christians?' an American visitor asked Brother Roberts as we sipped our cognac.

'Neither better nor worse,' he answered. 'Human nature is the same the world over. We get used to things, take them for granted.'

I, too, was getting used to Nazareth – the Nazareth that I saw with my eyes.

* * *

But there is another Nazareth. Nathaniel did not see it, and it is easy to miss it today.

We accept the Incarnation with our reason, believing that at a point in time less distant than the time of Pericles or Socrates or Julius Caesar, the Word was made Flesh. To accept it as a fact of history, or an intellectual concept, is one thing, to apprehend it another. At Nazareth it is hardly easier than elsewhere. I said: 'Here for thirty years the son of God lived in obscurity. . . . From this well his mother drew water. . . . Here was the synagogue from which they drove him forth. . . . From the brow of this hill they sought to cast him down.' I said these things, but did the words live?

The wind bloweth where it listeth. The spirit cannot be constrained. There were moments of realization, transitory, unattended. A sight commonplace in itself – a woman with a child, or a shepherd carrying a lamb – would take on a significance beyond itself, reaching to a truth that is eternal. . . . Once, too, I stood on the balcony outside my room. The midday light hung in a shimmering haze on a distance of parched earth and glaring limestone. The earth and the rocks were solid: a reality with which I was familiar. But in that moment, as the light struggling in the stillness of the noon changed the shapes of things familiar, I saw a different reality. Time was no more. For all time was gathered into the eternal Now of the Incarnation:

> '*Here the impossible union*
> *Of spheres of existence is actual,*
> *Here the past and future*
> *Are conquered and reconciled.*'

* * *

In the cave of the Annunciation at Nazareth two pillars of red porphyry mark the place of the Message of the Angel. Candles burn. Mass follows Mass. Princes have knelt in this place. The poor also come, and the old, and children.

CHAPTER XII

Places in Galilee

ABDULLAH was an ideal driver. All the times that he drove me in Galilee, now here, now there, he showed not a trace of impatience. He was content to go slowly, to wait interminably, to change plans at a moment's notice.

He would stop the car to let me look at a plant or tree or a shepherd dividing the sheep from the goats. Or we would watch oxen threshing: round and round they would go, treading the corn, their heads left free so that they could eat at will. 'Thou shalt not muzzle the ox that treadeth out the corn.' Sometimes the threshing was done by a horse pulling a sledge-like board the underside of which was fitted with pieces of flint or pointed iron – this is what Isaiah meant by a sharp instrument having teeth.

* * *

There was a horse threshing at Cana, in a field enclosed by a rough stone wall topped with a hedge of prickly-pear. Cana is a village of stone: squat stone houses and a street that turns sharply between stone walls. Hollyhocks grow there, and golden-red pomegranates. There is a church with geranium-coloured domes, and on the outskirts a well that moved the pilgrim Antonine of Piacenza to such devotion that he thought fit to have a bath in it!

I remember the church for a priest with a worried expression, who was at pains to make clear that a jar on view was NOT one of those used at the wedding feast when the water was turned into wine! In this church I had an uncomfortable feeling of being watched. The explanation was an ancient life-sized statue of a saint that stood in the gallery staring down out of the shadows.

* * *

Nein, at the foot of little Hermon, is a dead kind of place. A stony track leads up to it, and its houses, except for the Muktar's – which has an arched front and a certain elegance – are like little boxes made of stone or mud. There is a Moslem burial ground, and ancient Jewish tombs cut in the rock. They say it was to one of these that the body of the widow's son was being taken, when Christ, on his way from Nazareth, met the procession. . . . An Arab girl was stretched asleep on the steps into the church. Men dozed in doorways. A woman was standing by the well, waiting for the water to rise; she looked as if she had been standing there since the beginning of time.

* * *

From the plain of Esdraelon the road climbs Mount Tabor in hair-pin bends. On the top there is an arch called the Gate of the Winds; then a drive leading between cypress trees to a ruined abbey and the masonry of a Crusader fortress. Jasmine and oleanders bloom, and lizards dart among fragments of marble. The whole place is bathed in light. In the church of the Transfiguration light glows through arched amber windows.

* * *

The country between Nazareth and Safed has an especial beauty. At first it is open, with red mountains reaching away. Later the road runs through valleys and over hillsides thickly planted with olive trees, their foliage a metallic grey above the redness of the earth.

Abdullah stopped the car by a spring at which we drank ice-cold water. Then, again, to gather figs near a Druze village, where women went by wearing long white veils and men in white greeted us with solemn courtesy.

On the hillside at Meiron we came to the burial place of the Rabbis with its white domes and white-walled squares open to the sky. Here is buried Rabbi Simon Bar Yochai, one of the sages whose teaching inspired the Jewish revolt against the Romans. Gutted candles flickered on the tombs. An old man, bearded and wrinkled, came forward offering me a candle: I took it and put it with the others. Higher up is the cave-tomb of Rabbi Jochanan Hasandelar who, like Socrates, would accept no payment for his teaching: to make a living, he used to repair the sandals of his pupils. Here, too, is buried Rabbi Hillel, that gentle scholar, renowned through the ages for his interpretation of the Law. Higher up still stands a ruined synagogue. A huge monolith is supported by two columns with, on either side, walls built from large rough stones. The effect is one of simplicity and Cyclopean grandeur that brings to mind the Doric buildings of ancient Greece.

From Meiron you look across to Safed perched on the mountains, like a hill-town of the Apennines: it is, they tell you, the city of the gospels that was 'set on a hill'.

Safed is a place of tortuous lanes, steep flights of steps, white-washed houses with balconies and upper stories that jut out so that they meet across the street. Sephardi patriarchs in striped robes read yellow-leaved books in the cool quiet of synagogues decorated with mysterious cabbalistic signs. . . . The city is mentioned in an Egyptian papyrus that goes back fourteen hundred years before the birth of

Christ. Under the kingdoms of Israel and Judah it was called Tsafet, which means the 'place of outlook': from it beacons were relayed announcing the rising of the new moon which was proclaimed at Jerusalem.

Mount Canaan above Safed commands a view of special splendour. You see Hermon and the Sea of Galilee and, beyond, the plateau of Jordan with, at night, the twinkling lights of Dera'a. To the south-west are Nazareth and Tabor, Carmel and the sea.

* * *

A volcanic eruption gave birth to Hule; the little triangular lake that in the Bible they call the waters of Merom. For the Jordan, rushing on its way from the nymph-haunted cave of Banias and from the pools of Dan, was stayed in its course by lava, and, having no outlet, flooded the countryside. . . .

There it has lain through the centuries, more swamp than lake, hemmed in by mountains: the haunt of hyenas and jackals, buffaloes and wild boar; and, until recent times, the home of an Arab tribe who lived in reed tents, made mats and a red and black pottery that was simple and beautiful. Pierre Loti wrote of these Arabs: at night he saw the glow of their camp fires, but when he woke in the morning they were hidden in their tents among the reeds, like birds in their nests.

The Arabs are gone now, and the wild creatures are fewer. Great schemes are afoot whereby the marshes are being drained, and the Jordan's bed deepened and widened. Already swamps have given place to fertile fields. Yet, even so, Hule has not lost her strange, primeval atmosphere.

The boat slid over the green-clouded water, leaving a trail of silver in its wake. Ahead, as far as the eye could see, was green water; and on either side a jungle of bulrushes, tall rank grasses and tufted papyrus. The silence was of the jungle – tense, breathing, crowded; broken only by the purr of the engine, the cry of a bird or a stirring, felt rather than heard, in the reed-beds. On the mud at the water's edge, tortoises sunned themselves, so still and in colouring so like their surroundings that they might have been stones. Smyrna kingfishers, brilliant of plumage, perched motionless on reeds or streaked low over the water, flashing emerald and ultramarine. The larger, black and white kingfisher, shimmering like silk and graceful as a tern, hovered, then dived for its prey. Here, too, I saw skimming the water swallows whose breasts were flushed with rose.

CHAPTER XIII

The Sea of Galilee

WE DROVE south from Hule, and came to the Sea of Galilee in the evening, at that hour when the light seems to gather to itself all the splendour of the day.

The water spread below was a sheet of blue shining glass, reflecting in its depths the snow-splashed peak of Hermon and the creased, wine-shadowed mountains of Syria.

'This lake is better than Hule,' Abdullah remarked: I thought that he was referring to the landscape. Then he added: 'Because Our Lord walked on the water'.

Like Hule, the Sea of Galilee has mountains about it. To the east, the mountains of Syria, to the west the cave-riddled hills of Galilee crowned by twin-horned Hattim where Saladin routed the Crusaders, suffocating them in the smoke of burning thistles. But the resemblance to Hule ends there, for whereas the latter is lonely and primeval, Galilee has a gentle beauty and an air, almost, of sophistication. Its shape, too, is pleasing. It looks like a harp – and that is the meaning of the Hebrew name, Kinneret.

Its mood is unpredictable. At one moment the lake is as gay and smiling as Catullus' Sirmio. Then, with a suddenness past belief, a wind will sweep down from the mountains, churning the water, twisting and curling the waves, making them slap against the fishing boats' creaking hulls. 'Save us, Lord, for we perish,' Peter cried. The fishermen today have no less cause to fear.

* * *

'As he passed along the Sea of Galilee he saw Simon and Andrew his brother casting a net into the sea.' SAINT MATTHEW

Many a time, as you go along the side of the lake, you will see a man wade a few yards into the water, with arranged over his left arm a little net, its circular edge hung with pellets of lead. Keeping hold of the net's central cord and lifting his right arm, he casts it with a graceful throw. It opens like a parachute, then glides on to the surface of the water. Weighted by the lead it sinks to the bottom, imprisoning the catch. The man walks out and disentangles the fish; or, if the water is deep, recovers the net by drawing in the cord.

Or you may see a boat going out from the shore spreading the great *jarf* or drag-net. This is the net to which, in Saint Matthew's gospel, the kingdom of heaven is compared:

'The kingdom of heaven is like unto a net that was cast into the sea and gathered fish of every kind: which, when it was full, they drew to shore, and sat down, and gathered the good into vessels, but cast the bad away.'

This net is spread in a vast semicircle, the two ends being kept close to the shore. The upper part floats by means of corks, the lower is weighed down by lead. No sooner is it spread than men standing on the shore begin to haul it in. They do this with great care, for fear stones littering the bottom of the lake should tear the mesh.

Another net in common use is the *m'battan*. It is really three nets of equal size fastened to a pole. The two outer ones have a wide mesh, the inner one is fine. The fish, swimming through the large mesh, push the fine mesh through the holes of the net on the further side, and in doing so become entangled. More especially does this happen to the comb fish, which have long dorsal fins,

One variety of comb fish is called the fish of Saint Peter (*Chromis Simonis*) because in the mouth of one of these was found, so the story goes, the coin valuing four drachma exacted by the Roman treasury. The male fish carries its young in his mouth which becomes so distended as they grow that he can scarcely close it. How he feeds himself is a mystery.

There are also catfish, with enormous heads. These have no scales and in consequence may not be eaten by Orthodox Jews. They can survive on land an unusually long time, and are said to be able to move over dry ground. If taken hold of they give out a squeak.

After the first rains small fish belonging to the carp family, and called by the Arabs sardines, appear in the lake in great numbers. The Romans used to pickle these and export them to distant parts of the empire. Some think that the 'two small fishes' mentioned by Saint John were of this kind. Moreover, there is a tradition that John belonged to a family of fish merchants, who probably supplied fish to Caiaphas, the High Priest: this would explain why John was able to get Peter into the house of Caiaphas on the night that Jesus was betrayed.

Sardines are caught mostly at night. A light fastened to the boat helps to attract them.

* * *

In the time of the Romans, trees covered the whole of the country that is about the lake: the Emperor Vespasian found enough timber in the neighbourhood of Magdala to build a flotilla of warships. Moreover, Josephus remarked that trees so contrary in their needs as the palm and the walnut (the former needs heat, the latter air that is cool) flourished side by side. He described the region as the 'ambition' – perhaps we might say 'the dream' – of nature.

Today the mountains are bare and the vegetation confined to the low-lying ground about the lake. The great plain of Gennesareth is planted with vines and melons, citrus groves and bananas, the latter protected from the wind by screens made of matting. Palms and eucalyptus trees grow at Tiberias. There are a few palms, too, at Magdala, as well as figs, mimosa and sycamores.

At Tabgha eucalyptus trees shade the beach, and there is a grove with pools and cool clear streams and the remains of an ancient mill. Tabgha is the Arab name. The Greeks called the place Heptapegon, the seven springs, and Aetheira of Aquitania, a pilgrim of the fourth century, mentions a church of the same name built to commemorate the Feeding of the Five Thousand. Its altar was said to be of the stone on which the loaves and fishes had been laid. A mosaic floor is preserved: the design has a delicacy that is suggestive of Chinese art. Ducks and geese, storks and peacocks, are in a setting of oleanders, rushes and papyri. A heron fights a snake. A flamingo nibbles a blossom. Gaily coloured birds perch on lotus flowers. There is also an animal like a rabbit with a red ribbon round its neck.

There are trees at Capernaum, too. Eucalyptus trees and palms, tamarisks and sweet smelling firs, and, standing among the trees, the ruins of a synagogue that is like a classical temple. I was reminded of Olympia. To press the comparison would be absurd, for the synagogue is Roman not Greek in style. Yet the resemblance was there. The blue sky seen through green foliage that dappled the ruins with shadows. The grating sleepy note of cicadas. The ground strewn with marbles. The austerity inherent in classical buildings is seen to its best advantage in an austere setting. On the Acropolis at Athens. At Sunium. Among the parched hills about Jerash. Among trees this austerity is lost. A different, romantic quality is assumed. It is generally believed that the synagogue at Capernaum is built in part from the stones of the one in which Christ preached. Palm and acanthus leaves, grapes and pomegranates are among the decorations carved on it. There is also Solomon's star, and an elegant seven-branched candlestick.

Capernaum was on the ancient caravan route, later called the Via Maris, that ran between Damascus and the sea. At one of its toll-posts Matthew sat at the receipt of custom. It was one of many cities about the Sea of Galilee. There were nine in all. Capernaum, Hippos, Magdala, Gadara, Bethsaida, Taricheae, Gergesa, Chorazin, Tiberias. What now remains of these?

'Woe to thee Chorazin, woe to thee Bethsaida. . . . And thou Capernaum, dost thou hope to be lifted up as high as heaven? Thou shalt fall low as hell.'

They have become hardly more than names. Perhaps there is a mound of earth, or some broken marbles. Tiberias alone, is standing.

* * *

I have in my possession an old engraving of Tiberias. The white-domed town is visible below the blackened ruins of Herod's palace. Palms rise slim and feathery. Shadowy mountains drop to the water's edge. I saw Tiberias like this in the moonlight. By day it was less romantic. Yet, then, too, the domes and minarets, the trees and the flat-roofed houses, set there by the blue lake, made a pleasing picture. Great walls rose from the water and along the beach columns of basalt stood up like the trunks of trees. The heat was suffocating: I remember no cool, except in the little boat-shaped church built in honour of Saint Peter.

Tiberias has a strange history. It was founded by Herod Antipas who named it after the Roman Emperor. While it was being built, an ancient Jewish cemetery was disturbed, in consequence of which Herod so angered the Orthodox Jews that they boycotted the city. To populate it the King forcibly brought in people from the surrounding country, as well as foreigners, adventurers and beggars. Later, however, when Jerusalem fell to the Emperor Titus, Tiberias became a centre of Hebrew culture.

Pliny described the town as a health resort. '*Tiberiade aquis calidis salubre.*' And Josephus, who lead the Galileans in the war against Rome, said that John of Gisgala, one of the rebel leaders, visited the springs at Tiberias to recover his health. These springs are symbolized on a coin struck for the city during the reign of Tiberius. Hygeia, goddess of health, is depicted seated on a rock from which water gushes forth. She is giving food from a bowl to the serpent of Aesculapius, god of healing. The springs are still there, standing back from the lake, half a mile to the south of the town, with close to them the white domed tomb of Rabbi Meir.

* * *

The Mount of the Beatitudes slopes up from the lake with on its summit an Italian hospice run by Franciscan nuns.

Apart from two Franciscan fathers and a United Nations official, I was the only visitor. I ate my dinner at a solitary table in a great marbled refectory that was like the hall of an Italian palace. It was lit by electricity from high up on the walls, yet I used to feel as though I were sitting in candlelight. There were shadows and patches of darkness between pillars and, at the far end, a staircase sweeping up into more darkness. Through an open door into the garden

I could see a tangle of oleanders and palms and bamboos against the darkening sky. Sometimes a bat would flitter in, circle the pillars and be gone. The only sound was the murmur of the Franciscans, one of them thin and dark and tonsured, the other thick-set and Teutonic – sitting there opposite each other, fingering their grapes and sipping their wine.

The United Nations official sat alone near the door. He was a great gaunt man. In the evening he changed his khaki uniform for a cream linen jacket and a pair of bright blue trousers. At the end of dinner he was brought a pot of tea which he used to take outside, then settle himself in a camp chair, light a cigar and sit staring into the dusk. He rarely spoke except to ask one of the sisters for a jug of iced water. I used to meet him on the stairs carrying his jug. He was like one of those mysterious, silent characters that slip in and out of novels by Somerset Maugham.

My room had white walls and an iron bedstead standing high off the floor. A french window opened on to a loggia. Its wide roof was a protection against the sun, but it also kept out the air. The atmosphere was oppressive. Only at night would a faint breeze rise. I would hear it, stirring the bamboos. And, looking out on to the darkness of the lake, I would see the gliding solitary light of a fishing boat, and, in the distance, a cluster of lights that was Tiberias.

* * *

One morning instead of the country sounds to which I had become used – the braying of a donkey, turkeys gobbling, the crowing of cocks and the call of the bulbul birds – I woke to the shriek of brakes, the slamming of doors and a babel of French voices. Looking down from the loggia I saw three motor coaches and a swarm of people. They were pilgrims who were staying at Nazareth: they were to breakfast at the hospice, then make a tour of the holy places round the lake. It chanced that I already knew the man who had organized the outing. We had met in the English Bar. He asked me if I would like to go with the party to Capernaum.

A couple of hours later I was walking down the slope which tradition has associated with the Sermon on the Mount. It was parched by summer drought, and, where it reached down to the road bordering the lake, overgrown with thistles. Beyond the road the lake was a glittering sapphire.

I was with a priest from Chile: a leathery little man, swamped by an enormous sun-helmet. Like myself, he was not one of the pilgrims, but had been invited to join the party. Conversation was limited, since the only language we could find in common was Latin. Every now and then he would stand still, remove his helmet, take out a handkerchief and wipe his brow.

The rest of the party had gone ahead in the buses and were already at Capernaum when we arrived. They were sitting under the trees among the ruins of the synagogue or on the broken millstones and drums of pillars that littered the ground – as motionless as the stones about them. In the middle a young man, wearing the white habit of a Dominican and on his head a *keffiyeh*, stood reading aloud from the gospel according to Saint John.

'*Je suis le pain de vie. Vos pères ont mangé la manne dans le désert, et ils sont morts. Mais voici le pain qui est descendu du ciel, afin que celui qui en mange ne meure point. Je suis le pain vivant qui suis descendu du ciel.*'

So had Christ spoken here in the synagogue at Capernaum: and hearing his words many of his disciples walked with him no more.

We scrambled into the buses and drove back in the direction from which we had come, as far as the little church of the Primacy of Peter. I imagined that we were going to crowd into it, to stare at the huge brown rock that sprawls in front of the altar. I was mistaken. A mood of gaiety had taken hold of the party. Their one wish, now, was to bathe. Not that piety and bathing could not go together. Was not this the Sea of Galilee? Had not Christ stilled these waves? Was it not on these shores, if not on this very spot, that he had appeared to his disciples after the Resurrection, eaten broiled fish with them, bidden Peter 'Feed my lambs, feed my sheep'. . . . The party, what with the associations of the place and delight at the shimmering water, was no less moved, no less excited, than those pilgrims of old who used to face discomfort and danger if only they might plunge into the Jordan, or, at least, dip hand or foot in its blessed waters.

In less than minutes the beach was strewn with bathing kit or with discarded garments of those already in the lake. There was splashing and laughter and shouting. Some who did not bathe paddled at the water's edge – among them the priest from Chile, his soutane hitched above his pale legs. Others sat under the eucalyptus trees, where fishing nets were hanging to dry – the women knitting and chattering, the men shouting words of encouragement or mockery to those in the water. The Dominican who at Capernaum had been reading the gospel, was sitting on a rock, a towel slung about his neck. Drops of moisture glistened on his tousled hair and sun-burned back. I could not but smile at the thought of that other Dominican, Brother Felix, who, while bathing naked in the Jordan, saw a fellow pilgrim almost drowned. Shaken by what had occurred, he began to reflect how the mishap might have happened to himself.

'It seemed unbearable', he wrote, 'that I should sink in the water without my habit. With my habit I would not have minded so much.' So great was his compunction for his frivolous behaviour, that on his next visit to the Jordan he was content, instead of swimming, to sit up to his neck in shallow water, wearing his shirt and scapular.

CHAPTER XIV

Haifa and Mount Carmel

I

THE HISTORY of Haifa is linked with Crusader times. A Crusader seal going back to 1250 shows the governor in knight's armour, mounted on horseback. South of the city, on the rocky headland of Atlit, stands the Crusader castle that was called the *Castra peregrinorum*. Pilgrims knew the city as Caifa, and surmised that it was named after the High Priest Caiphas.

In earlier times there was a little port, lying in the shelter of Mount Carmel, where Greek settlers made glass and purple dye. Its Jewish community, influenced no doubt by their contact with foreigners, was criticized for pronouncing their Hebrew carelessly and, for this reason, debarred from officiating in the synagogues or reading the Torah in public. After the destruction of the city by Saladin, Acre took its place in importance, but Jews living in Acre used to take their dead to Haifa for burial because the former were regarded as being outside the bounds of the Holy Land.

All this was long ago. Today Haifa is Israel's largest port. For this reason, and perhaps also by the nature of her history, she is more extrovert in character, more open to outside influences, than either Jerusalem or Tel Aviv. . . . There are, too, more Arabs in the streets than elsewhere, especially the Druzes – that dignified, secretive people who maintain their traditions and religious beliefs in villages scattered over the heights of Carmel or further afield in Galilee.

Haifa on the level of the sea is a place of shipping and commerce. Docks, warehouses, customs sheds, a maritime museum, a seamen's union – all, in fact, that makes up the world of a port – are set about a harbour crowded with liners and merchant vessels, gunboats and launches, fishing smacks, barges, cattle boats and tugs. An enormous grain silo towers to the sky, with further inland business houses and shops, some of them built in the Arab tradition of arches and strong thick walls. On the Jaffa road there is a German hospice with a laid-out garden full of palms and vines, rosemary bushes and giant hollyhocks.

From this lower level the city climbs higher and higher up the slopes of Carmel. Stores, blocks of flats, municipal buildings stand one above the other, interspersed by parks and gardens. Villas and hotels, schools and synagogues and churches rise out of the green of cypresses. The dome on the shrine of the Bab glitters with gold. On the summit the Carmelite monastery looks out over a vast bay sweeping northward to where in the Lebanon the sun falls in shafts of silver on cliffs that are called the Ladders of Tyre. At night the lights along the coast and reaching inland up the sides of the mountain are like jewels showered upon the darkness.

II

Carmel juts out into the sea, but extends inland too, in a great solid ridge, twenty miles long, as far as the plain of Esdraelon. You see that huge range from Nazareth, from Jaffa, from the hills of Samaria, from Hermon, from the lands of Gila'ad east of the Jordan. In a country that is scorched and arid, Carmel is clothed with trees: the name means a garden. 'Thine head upon thee is like Carmel' the writer of the Canticle says to his beloved. For Isaiah Mount Carmel is a figure of the lavish goodness of God: should the trees on Carmel droop, that indeed were a sign of God's displeasure: an image of unutterable desolation. For Micah, the pastures of Carmel are an emblem of the loving care that God bestows upon his people. 'Feed thy sheep with thy rod', says the prophet, 'the flock of thine heritage which dwell solitarily in the forest in the midst of Carmel'.

Almost from the beginning of time, Carmel has been a sanctuary, a place where man, withdrawing from the world, has sought communication, however dimly, with his Creator. In the fifth century before Christ a divine being was reputed to dwell upon the mountain. Pythagoras the philosopher came here to meditate.

Tacitus wrote: 'Between Syria and Judea is Carmel – the name given to the mountain and to a god. Yet, there is no image to the god nor any temple, but only, as former ages prescribed, an altar and worship. Vespasian sacrificed there when revolving in his mind the yet secret hope of empire.'

No image to the god? To a Roman that might well seem strange, but the God worshipped on Carmel was not a pagan deity, not the anthropomorphic conception of the human mind. He was the true God, revealed alone to the Children of Israel, his Chosen People – a god whose image might not be graven in stone. His worship was vindicated by the prophet Elijah, who, having brought drought upon the earth, called down fire from heaven and slew the priests of Baal at the foot of Carmel, by the brook Kishon. And after he had killed the priests, Elijah went up on to the top of the mountain, and, casting himself upon the earth, bade his servant go and look out towards the sea. When the servant came and said that he had seen nothing, the prophet told him to go back seven times. And at the seventh time a little cloud, the size of the palm of a man's hand, rose out of the sea. 'And, behold, the heavens grew dark with clouds and wind and there fell great rain.'

The early Christian hermits who withdrew to Mount Carmel were the spiritual descendants of Elijah. They lived on the heights of the mountain in cells that looked like beehives, making, through a life of prayer and contemplation, a 'sweet, spiritual honey'. In the year 1212 Saint Brocard, born in the Holy Land of French parents, gathered together those who were of the Latin rite and obtained for them a rule from Albert, Patriarch of Jerusalem.

Such was the origin of the monks of the Carmelite Order.

But their life of untroubled contemplation was not to last. Attacks by the Saracens were constant. In 1238 a number of the monks were massacred as they stood, with lighted candles in their hands, singing the *Salve Regina.* After the siege of Acre still more of them were murdered and their buildings devastated. Those who survived had to abandon the mountain.

Nearly four hundred years later, in 1631, Father Prospero du Saint Esprit, a Carmelite of Spanish descent returned to Mount Carmel with two companions and, despite dangers and opposition, restored monastic life.

The following century the monastery was rebuilt. Napolean used it as a hospital for his wounded and plague-stricken soldiers. But scarcely had he left the country when both monks and soldiers were murdered and the buildings destroyed.

The present monastery, which goes back to 1834, stands on the mountain's north-westerly point high above the sea. It looks like a great fortress. Walls are thick, windows barred. Enclosed in it, to be secure against the onslaught of enemies, is the basilica dedicated to Our Lady of Mount Carmel, built over a cave where the prophet Elijah is said to have lived.

Above the cave a cedar-wood statue of Christ's Mother is enthroned. In her hand she bears the scapular that is the token of her love. For love has crowned the old austerity. On Carmel a new flower has bloomed.

CHAPTER XV

Kibbutzim

I

THE KIBBUTZIM are the pride of Israel. Everyone talks about them. 'Have you visited a *kibbutz*?' 'Are you going to stay on a *kibbutz*?' I was asked a hundred times.

The *Kibbutz* Mizra was on the plain of Esdraelon. On this plain Barak pursued the chariots of Sisera, and Gideon, gathering three hundred warriors, did battle against the hosts of Midian. Here, at the foot of Gilboa Saul was slain, and Jonathan his son. . . .

The large dining room was airy and full of sunshine, with pink walls and light-coloured furniture. Men and women sat at long tables, or moved about pushing trolleys and serving the food from aluminium containers. Most of them wore blue shorts – a few older women were in cotton dresses. There was a roar of voices. Soup was put in front of me, then rissoles and gravy, tomatoes, cucumber and lentils, followed by fruit and cheese with coarse-grained brown bread. There was a drink made from apples.

'When we came here we found nothing but stones and mud.' The woman who was showing me round spoke English carefully, but with a monotonous intonation as though she were repeating a lesson. 'That is how it was with most of the *kibbutzim* in the beginning. Settlers came from Russia, Poland, Lithuania, the Ukraine. They cleared the stones, drained the swamps, planted fields and orchards.'

We went out into the sun, across a lawn planted with

saplings, then into a one-storied house built of concrete. The room was dark because the shutters were closed, but I could see that, though small, it was pleasantly furnished.

'This is our room, my husband's and mine,' she said.

'And the children?' I asked, for she had previously told me that there were three.

'They are in the children's houses. They come to us daily for a couple of hours, after tea until their bed-time. Sometimes I put the little one to bed myself.'

We walked across to the children's houses. A little girl (she looked perhaps eight or nine) lay on a bed in a shaded room with two others, also lying on their beds. She reached up her arms to her mother, and there was a conversation in Hebrew. 'She wants to know who you are, where you come from,' her mother told me, 'what is your work?'

We went on to another house for smaller children. They were having showers before their afternoon rest: the water streamed down their sunburnt naked bodies. Then to another where boys sat at a table, some reading, others playing chess.

'We bring them up to be responsible members of a community,' my escort said.

'But do they see enough of their parents?' I asked.

'But of course.' There was a touch of impatience in her voice: the upbringing of children in the *kibbutzim* is a subject of controversy even in Israel. 'I have explained they see their parents every evening and all day on the Sabbath. In fact they see more of them than do the children of city workers. And at the time when the parents are relaxed and able to give of their best. The rest of the time they are looked after by experts, and have the company of other children.'

I thought it a cold, impersonal upbringing: a poor substitute for the natural day-to-day and hour-to-hour relationship between child and parent that is the essence of family life. Perhaps she sensed my thoughts, for she said 'It's strange for the British to criticize us for this – with your boarding schools.'

I said nothing. But I knew that I was not alone in feeling as I did. The system at Mizra is common in Israel. Yet it is not the only one. At Ein Harod, for example, the parents have their children to live with them from the age of six, while at S'de Eliahu, an Orthodox settlement, many of the houses built for married couples have rooms for children. In the early days of the *kibbutzim* children were cared for apart from their parents to enable women to work in the fields along with the men. What was in the beginning a temporary and, to a large extent, necessary measure, has become accepted as permanent and good – especially in settlements founded under the influences of *Mapam*, the extreme left wing party.

'Under our system,' my companion went on, 'a woman can work without anxiety. She knows that her children are cared for by responsible persons. It is the same with regard to one's husband. Last week my husband was not well. I could go out in the morning knowing he would be cared for – that his meals would be brought, that there was a doctor to visit him.

'Anyone who is ill in a *kibbutz* is looked after. We had a boy with cancer. He was taken to hospital, given the best treatment. The *kibbutz* supplies the money. We have no money of our own. We work for the *kibbutz*, not for individual gain. Our clothes and food are given to us. So is our furniture.'

'Have you a choice in such things?'

'Yes, within reason, and within the capacity of the *kibbutz*. We don't expect luxury, and we don't get it. But we can choose up to a point – the colour, for instance, of our curtains and covers. In our room there is a writing desk because I need it – I am a teacher of English.'

The conversation came back to the children.

'They have a general education here on the *kibbutz*, with an emphasis, of course, on agriculture. Most of them, boys and girls, after their military service, come back, marry and settle down. But they are not compelled to come back. If someone has a bent, say, for one of the professions, the *kibbutz* will raise the money for the training. But what Israel needs is farmers: there are plenty of professional people. And we want farming done in the modern way. Experts from America help us, and exchange visits are arranged with other countries. A boy who went from here to Switzerland found the methods there old-fashioned!'

We passed hay-ricks, and a byre full of fine-looking cattle, then stopped to drink ice-cold water from a billy-can.

'Is this your model of what a *kibbutz* should be? Do you visualize the Oriental immigrants living like this some day?'

She hesitated. 'I don't know,' she said. 'The Orientals don't understand co-operation as we do.'

One comes up constantly against the problem of the Oriental immigrants; the difficulty of their adapting themselves to western ways. This is especially so in regard to the Moroccans. They are, one is told, aggressive, resentful, untruthful and lazy: the children have been known to go to the lengths of trying to stone, or knife, their educators. Wherever the immigrants come from, whatever the colour of their skin, they are one in that they are Jews. But in practice the 'one-ness' is hard to realize. A gulf separates the Moroccan or Indian from the Jew of the west. Israel is run on western lines with the result that up to the present the majority of responsible posts have inevitably gone to European Jews. 'There is racial discrimination here, too,'

I heard a youth declaim in a Tel Aviv café. The western-minded Jew tends, like most Europeans, to think of his brothers and sisters from the east as being childish and primitive, if not illiterate. The problem, too, of educating the Oriental is increased by the fact that his mind is unlike that of the west: he does not understand abstract ideas. To give one instance, Yemenite children, untouched by western influences, can make nothing of maps – yet their zeal for learning is phenomenal.

My companion was full of admiration for the Yemenites.

'If all the immigrants were like them, there would be no problem,' she said. 'They are industrious, intelligent and grateful for what is done for them.'

I asked if there was a synagogue in the *kibbutz*. 'No,' she answered, 'we are not religious. . . . But we have a cultural centre. . . . Lectures, music and plays, and, of course, the radio and the cinema.'

We went into a hall with wood panelling and open glass doors. Paintings were on show, by a member of the *kibbutz*. He had done them over a period of fourteen years in the time left over from the farm work. Many were country scenes: they had a fresh, restful quality, whereas, much of the painting and sculpture that I saw in Israel had a crude violence which brought to mind certain aspects of modern Scandinavian art.

Before I left, I asked my escort if she wanted sometimes to get away from the community life. 'I don't think so,' she told me, 'I like it. You must remember that no one is compelled to stay. Those who don't like it, or aren't suited, don't stay. . . . You must remember, too, that we get a holiday. The *kibbutz* gives us money and we go away for a week, or perhaps two weeks, in the year.'

Abdullah was waiting. We drove out between hedges of

cypresses, then on to the main road. A train of camels was going by ridden by Arabs. A donkey was leading. In the distance the stone, square-built houses of Nazareth rested against the hills.

II

Within a week I was travelling north from Haifa with Mr S. I was to spend a couple of nights with friends of his at the *Kibbutz* Eilon.

Leaving behind suburbs and oil refineries and factories, the jeep rattled along the flat straight road with ahead the mountains of Lebanon, and to the left the blue line of the sea. We came to the River Naaman which the Greeks used to call the Belus. It was here, so Pliny records, that some shipwrecked sailors made the first transparent glass.

Suddenly, there were palm trees rising from a waste of sandy ground, and, visible through the trees, domes and minarets and flat white buildings glittering in the sunlight. It was Acre. In that moment Israel seemed far away. I was looking at an Arabian Nights city. A place of legend and poetry. A mirage, perhaps.

We turned seawards, leaving behind a Moslem cemetery with its desolation of crowded stones. Most of them were horizontal with a vertical stone at either end – like bedsteads. They looked as if they had been flung there, haphazard – as though it were a place not where the dead were sleeping, but rather one they had abandoned hurriedly, finding there no rest.

I walked through the city's zigzagging streets as in a dream. Not even the cheerful companionship of Mr S. could give me an assurance of reality. My footsteps echoed under a great arched gateway. I gazed at merchandise in the shadowy vaulted bazaars, and at coppersmiths beating out their trays. I stopped to stare at a *sabeel*, or drinking fountain, of delicate workmanship enclosed in a bronze cage. Near it rounded steps led up to a gate that was painted white and ornamented with green and grey and black. Inside was a vast courtyard – it, too, staring white in the brilliant sunlight and planted with palms and little orange trees. In the middle stood the mosque of Jezzar, with its splendid domed roof and at the door two twisted pillars. Close by was a minaret and a sundial. Enclosing the courtyard, there were buildings with graceful arcades and little domes that looked like mushrooms. The atmosphere was one of peace and dignity.

An old man wearing deep-seated trousers and a *tarbush* swathed with white and gold went ahead of us into the mosque, his brown feet moving silently over the marble floor. It was cool and spacious. A bluish-green light hung upon it. Arabesques in blue and green and black decorated the walls. Through the deep-set, barred windows I could see the orange trees in the sleepy sun-drenched court.

We made our way to the harbour where great bastions jutted into a sea that broke languidly on dark rocks with tops strangely flat, as if they had been sliced across. This was the Acre of Saladin and the Crusaders, of Richard the Lion-Hearted. Saint John of Acre, they called it. Here Saint Francis landed.

Acre was, indeed, like a dream.. But one from which I was to be rudely awakened. After hardly more than a glance at the splendid harbour we had to be on our way again. It was the eve of the Sabbath. The driver of the jeep was determined to get Mr S. back to Haifa before sundown. As it was he was disgruntled at our having stopped. But if

Jerusalem: the Via Dolorosa

Jerusalem: the Dome of the Rock

he was disgruntled, I was more so. To cut short Acre for the sake of a *kibbutz* seemed to me unbearable.

* * *

On to the north. The flat straight road. To the west, glimpses of sand and sea. Ahead the mountains – shadows upon them gave them a grim, fierce look. I began to feel apprehension as to what might await me at the end of my journey, for only now had I discovered that Mr S. had not warned his friends of my arrival.

We had turned inland. The road curved upward among the mountains. I looked back at the sea, glittering in the evening light, like a great silver shield. The landscape was lonely and treeless, but with, here and there, a well-tended vineyard.

We drove through a gate past some large shining tractors. There was the usual water tower and small pink-roofed houses, many of them with a garden in front. I said that I would wait in the jeep. It would be better, I thought, for Mr S. to see his friends alone: if they did not want a visitor, they could say so more easily. The driver was more sulky than ever: he was smoking a cigarette with jerky, angry puffs. Presently Mr S. came back with a red rose in his hand. He held it out to me. 'You are welcome', he said.

* * *

I sat eating water melon and grapes in the little house occupied by Mr and Mrs T. There was one small room simply furnished, and off it a kind of pantry with next to this a shower room. Adjoining the house was a similar one for another married couple.

Mr T. was a great tall man with springy straw-coloured hair and cornflower-blue eyes that matched his shirt. His wife was the daughter of a German poet who had devoted the greater part of his life to working for the Zionist Movement. She was stocky and broad-shouldered with neat features and eyes grey as marbles under clearly defined brows. Her face wore that look of gravity that I have seen on the faces of Quakers.

I was accepted, made welcome. Yet I felt embarrassed. Mr T., it transpired, was going to sleep in one of the houses for unmarried men so that I might share the room with his wife. It was of no consequence, I was assured; such things were taken for granted in a *kibbutz*.

It was the end of the day. The children were in and out visiting their parents. A son of fifteen, well-built and fair-haired, with a friendly, open countenance. A younger son, dark and reserved in manner, keeping a distance. Little Naomi, her flaxen curls tied in scarlet ribbons, her eyes the colour of her father's, her plump legs showing brown below blue shorts. She said something to me in Hebrew, then put into my hands crayon drawings she had made of flowers and farm animals.

It was a few minutes walk to the communal dining room. As at Mizra I was conscious of a roar of voices and a clatter of crockery. But the room was smaller and shabbier. We sat three on either side of a table covered with oilcloth, so close that our elbows touched. Next to me was a dark heavily-built girl – evidently an Oriental – drinking *leben* in deep concentration, her arms resting on the table. A swarthy young man opposite asked if it was my first visit to a *kibbutz*. When I said I had been to Mizra, interest was roused and others joined in the conversation, for the two *kibbutzim* belong to the same political ideology. Much of the talk was in Hebrew and interpreted by the man who first spoke. They were anxious, he told me, to know about the dining room at Mizra and were hoping, when they could afford it, to have a similar one.

There was no waiting on ceremony. People helped themselves (I soon saw that I was expected to do the same), stretching across the table and often talking with their mouths full. They ate quickly, and when they had finished took up their cups and plates and put them on a trolley. Through an open door I could see clouds of steam, and men and girls washing dishes.

I knew that many of those around me were intellectuals from Germany: writers, lawyers, doctors, people who before Hitler's persecution had lived in an atmosphere of leisure and culture. I found myself wondering whether they disliked – at least some of them – this shoulder-to-shoulder community life. Did they accept it merely as something to be endured for the sake of a higher good?

As time went on, would they and their children lose all sense of the grace of living? Or would a reaction set in? After all, as well as the *kibbutzim*, there were in Israel other settlements of a different kind, where, though the land and farm implements and animals were shared in common, people lived with their children in homes of their own.

We went out past groups of young men, some talking excitedly, others reading the news-sheet which the *kibbutz* issued on a Friday evening. The night was cool. A breeze blew down from the mountains. The long leaves of the eucalyptus trees swayed against the stars. Music from a wireless drifted across the stillness. Lights shone in open doorways and uncurtained windows. 'There isn't much privacy,' Mrs T. said to me: it was the only shadow of criticism that I heard during my visit.

* * *

I woke early to country sounds: the lowing of a cow; birds twittering; the gobbling of turkeys. Through the window I could see trees and, beyond them, mountains that were a dark, slate grey, with here and there a streak of emerald. Mrs T.'s bed was a few feet from mine. She was still asleep, humped under the sheet, her dark hair spread on the pillow. It was the Sabbath: the only day on which she could rest. I, too, turned over and slept.

There was no synagogue, no religious observance of the Sabbath. But there was a slackening of pace, a sense of leisure. The children were about: they swam in the pool and played games. The boys gathered excitedly around a new brightly painted lorry. A hose was spraying the gardens in front of the houses – on other days the water had to be kept for the crops and the vines. At mid-day Mr T. came back from the fields. He brought out sweet corn and bunches of grapes from his knapsack. The children stood around him watching: the little girl clapped her hands.

* * *

'Well, do you like it?' A man wearing spectacles asked me, as I looked at the apple and pear trees, the strawberry bed, the lavender and the roses.

'I do,' I said.

'And so you ought.' His tone was aggressive, as though I had said, or was about to say, something unfavourable.

'We're not peasants,' he went on, in a tone still aggressive, but less so. 'The people who settled here were not farmers, yet they turned to this. . . . You think of the Jews as financiers and traders' – he was no longer aggressive; he was explaining – 'the Jews weren't traders, weren't urban, until they were exiled from their own country. They were forced into trade, forced into handling money by their lords and masters who would not allow them to own land. In their own country they had lived by the soil, and on the soil. And now they are going back to the soil, going back to what is their salvation. Collective farming is our salvation, racially and individually. But we can't farm individually – we haven't the money or the implements – we couldn't survive.'

'Ideally,' I asked, 'do you want all Jews to come back to Israel?'

'We want more and more. We want brains, talent. Some of the people who have these are the ones who don't come.' His words brought to my mind a young Zionist at a settlement outside Jerusalem: he had been talking of the help coming from America: 'They give their money,' he said, 'but they won't give themselves'.

'But is there room for so many?' I asked.

'Room?' His tone was impatient. 'We make room. We turn rock into soil. We drain swamps, take water into the desert. . . . There were settlers by the Dead Sea who washed the salt out of the soil and grew tomatoes!' His eyes were lit with enthusiasm. 'Give us the men and the women,' he went on. 'We'll make the soil. We did it here. We settled when it was an area forbidden to Jews and cut off by barbed wire. We forced our way in, lived in tents and huts, in mud and swamp. Look at us now. The *kibbutz* is self-supporting. And when the children born here grow up and go away for their military service, they come back and settle. What better advertisement?'

I was among people fanatical in their devotion to an ideal – pioneers who had staked their claim to their land, then held to it tooth and nail. They were a people bound to one another in a compact of endurance, thrown back upon their own resources. Outside themselves, they could look to no security, no refuge. Theirs was a border settlement.

If an attack were to come, it was for them to save their soil. At night they kept watch in turns. There were times, too, when they carried arms as they tilled the ground.

* * *

I walked with Mrs T. over slopes planted with vines that were weighed down by immense clusters of green and purple grapes. We each picked a bunch, rinsed it under a tap and ate as we went along.

I was welcome, and yet an intruder. Mrs T., knowing that I was writing a book, looked on me, not without justification, as someone who had come to pick up information to be used as 'copy'.

'You can't understand a *kibbutz* in a week-end,' she said, as we looked around the factory where they were making tractors.

'I can't,' I agreed. 'But I hope I can learn something.'

'A journalist came here,' she continued, 'then went away and wrote nonsense, thinking she knew everything.'

We passed hen-houses full of white wyandots. Then little blue bee-hives: the sky above them was full of bright-coloured whirring birds.

It was dusk as we went into the enclosure where the children's animals were kept. I could just see the donkey's ears and head, and feel its breath upon my hand. Rabbits pressed their noses against the wire of their hutch. A goose honked. We walked back with Naomi to the children's house. At the door, she flung her arms about her mother, then darted in. Through a window I saw small children sitting at a table made to suit their size. An elderly woman was helping them to soup. As we were going a tiny child ran out. '*Abba, abba*,' she cried. Her father turned back, bent down and caught her into his arms.

III

In the wilderness the Children of Israel murmured against Moses, for they remembered the flesh-pots of Egypt, the fish and the melons, the cucumbers and onions and leeks. And Moses, having spoken with God, kept them there, wandering in the wilderness for forty years, allowing only their children to enter the Promised Land. . . .

In the newer *kibbutzim* there are those in middle age who, loyal Zionists as they are, yet look back with nostalgia to the way of life they knew before they settled in Israel. Their children, troubled by no such longings, grow weary hearing their parents talk of better days: this sometimes makes for tension and a split between the generations.

Degania, founded in 1911, has the advantage of having a middle-aged generation born and bred there. This, along with the fact that the settlement is large enough (there are over two thousand members) to absorb conflicting opinions instead of being torn assunder by them, makes for stability. There is a more normal approach to living. Children, for the most part, sleep in the houses of their parents. Religion is not looked at askance: those so inclined attend a near-by synagogue, keep the feasts and the days of fasting.

'We don't expect everyone to live on a *kibbutz* . . . nor every Jew to return to Israel,' Joseph Baratz said to me, smiling under his floppy white hat. They call him the 'father of Degania'. He came to Israel from the Ukraine as a very young man, was there at the settlement's foundation, saw it grow to maturity. He has no axe to grind – he takes you over the *kibbutz* with a quiet confidence, like a landowner showing his estate.

Degania (the name means cornflower) is at the southern

end of the Sea of Galilee, where the Jordan leaves the lake on its way to the Dead Sea. The first settlers found a region of stifling heat and malarial swamp. The heat is still intense (the valley is below sea-level), but I was surprised that it was not even more violent. There were beds of bright flowers, orchards and cypresses, little glades of eucalyptus and pepper trees, and, through the trees, the lake and the Jordan's green waters.

CHAPTER XVI

The Old City: I

Urbs caelestis, urbs beata,
Supra petram collocata,
Urbs in portu satis tuto,
De longinquo te saluto,
Te saluto, te suspiro,
Te affecto, te requiro.

HILDEBERT

IN ISRAEL I had looked across at the walls of the Old City shimmering in the mid-day sun. At times their beauty had mocked me. They seemed hardly to be made of stone. Were they a dream, I asked myself? A façade, perhaps, to delight the eye, but with no more solidity than a painted scene upon the stage?

Now, I was inside those walls.

When I was a child, I saw, once, an old print of a city with great bastions enclosing a multitude of people of different races and colours. Written on it were the words, *Civitas Dei*. That was the city in which I now found myself.

I made my way through the street that runs south from the Damascus Gate. It was narrow and crowded. Many were in eastern dress. The men wore the long cotton tunic. Over this some wore the *abayah*, which is a woollen outer garment – a kind of cloak, decorated with, perhaps, gold or silver thread, and hanging in loose graceful folds. The women were in black embroidered with colours that were bright but never garish. All walked with that dignity of carriage that is too often lost when eastern dress gives place to that of the west. Donkeys blocked the way, so laden that sometimes only a head and ears were visible. A huge Ethiopian monk towered above me. A porter in a tunic of sacking, bent double under half-a-dozen sewing machines, thrust by with a shout: '*Oo-ha, oo-ha ya wajak!*' ('Look out for your face!'). A sherbet-seller tinkled his brass dishes. A water-carrier with an animal's skin for a bottle cried: '*Ya atsheneen, ya atsheneen!*' ('All ye who thirst. . . !').

The street led into the covered *souk* which was like a tunnel, its darkness lit from time to time by shafts of sunlight coming through openings in the roof. There was a smell of garlic and cooking and humanity. Open-fronted shops, reaching back like caves, displayed loaves and cakes, pastry and boiled sweets; sacks full of flour and sugar and lentils; baskets of peppers, beetroots, potatoes and tomatoes; live rabbits and poultry and pigeons. Eggs hung outside in metal containers. Pink earthenware pots, the colour of the soil round Jerusalem, stood on the pavement.

A tablet in the wall of the *souk* marked the Seventh Station of the Cross. Long ago there was a gate here, leading out of the city: Nehemiah mentioned it as being between the Fish Gate on the north and the Gate of Ephraim on the south. Here Christ fell on the way to Calvary.

I went on, then up a ramp to the right and past a shop that sold jugs and coffee pots made of brass, ikons, beads and mother-of-pearl rosaries, and crosses carved out of olive wood. Before me was an arched gateway leading into the courtyard of the church of the Holy Sepulchre.

* * *

I felt as if I had come to the end of a journey. I might make other journeys, and see things more spiendid. Yet here, in this candlelit Tomb, was the consummation of all things. Here Christ's body had lain, from here he had risen from the dead. They were right, those geographers of medieval times who had believed that the centre of the world was in this place, within the church of the Holy Sepulchre.

The church was dark, but the tomb was filled with a warm light. It came from flickering tapers and gilded ikons and the lamps hanging above the marble slab that hides the rock on which Christ's body lay. A bowed figure in a shabby patched cloak was kneeling at the slab. His dark-skinned face was furrowed with age, and lit with joy. He leant forward and kissed the slab again and again, murmuring softly. I knelt down at his side and laid my hand on the marble. It was smooth and cold and a great crack ran across it.

Marble covers the rock. There are walls of marble and a marble roof, and, beyond these and enclosing them, the walls of the church and the dome above the rotunda. For the church of the Holy Sepulchre is, as it were, a *tabernaculum* that has sheltered Calvary and the place of the Resurrection from the onslaught of enemies and the ravages of time. There are those who complain that marble should hide the hill on which the Cross stood and the simple rock-hewn Tomb. Some, rejecting the tradition of the ages, have sought another Calvary, another Tomb. Yet this church, reaching back in time to the finding of the True Cross by Helena, mother of Constantine – battered though it has been through the centuries, broken and built again – alone can give us an assurance of the place of the Crucifixion and whence it was that the glory of the risen Christ shone forth on the first Easter Sunday.

I bowed my head as I went out through the low doorway. It is so low, that when Mass is said in the Tomb you will see the serving boy lay his hand upon the head of the priest that he may not knock it against the lintel as he passes in and out, bent almost double. I was in the outer chamber now, the chapel of the Angel – so named because there is preserved a piece of rock on which, so it is said, the Angel sat on Easter morning. From here I went into the darkness of the church.

It was not just darkness that is the absence of light – as in some great empty basilica. This was a crowded darkness full of shapes that jutted out, then fell back melting into yet deeper darkness. There were screens and arches and galleries, scaffolding, props and girders. Pillars loomed suddenly, like trees in a fog. From somewhere out of the darkness, that was dank and smelling of wax and oil and incense, came the strange wild chanting of Greek monks, at once melancholy and triumphant, discordant perhaps to western ears, yet beautiful.

I passed between two pillars supported by scaffolding and found myself by the Stone of Unction which marks the place where Christ's body was annointed for burial. Women knelt in front of it, their long veils showing white in the shadows. Over it hung a row of pale, cloudy looking lamps. I was near the door of the church now. Inside it there was a shabby divan belonging to the Moslems, who keep the key – a privilege that has been in one family since the time of Suleiman the Magnificent. A few yards from where I stood, a flight of steps lead up in pitchy darkness to Calvary. The steps were steep and worn and of different sizes. At the top, lamplight flickered on the gold of the mosaics in the Latin chapel of the Nailing to the Cross. On a line with this, past a shrine to Our Lady of Sorrows, was the chapel of the Greeks, its altar built over the rock upon which the Cross stood. It was full of warmth and mystery, lights and shifting shadows. Gold and silver glittered. Lamps glowed in front of ikons. Tapers burned. Red shining balls hung from the ceiling. Life-sized figures of Mary and Saint John, in gold and silver, stood either side a gold and silver Christ upon the Cross. A black-robed monk kept watch. There was a hushed coming and going. Young and old. The people of Jerusalem. Pilgrims. Tourists. They lit tapers, knelt on the marble floor, kissed the place of the Cross. A few stared, not comprehending what it was they looked upon.

The darkness deepened. The silence became more intense.

Blake, when asked whether at sunrise he did not see a round disk of fire somewhat like a guinea, replied. 'Oh no, no, I see an Innumerable Company of the Heavenly Host crying, "Holy, Holy, Holy, is the Lord God Almighty." ' For him, his corporeal eye was no more than a window. 'I look through and not with it,' he said. . . . The church of the Holy Sepulchre is dim and battered and shabby. It is held together by scaffolding, struts and girders. There are tawdry hangings, dusty chandeliers, glass balls, artificial flowers and a clutter of pictures, many of them not in the best of taste. Along with the true holy places, there are gathered into it, places sacred – if sacred at all – only through legend or pious memory. All this is true. And this may be all you will see. For men see what they want to see and what they look for they find. So it is with the Holy Sepulchre. Those who look beyond the dust and the trappings will find a place of love: God's love out-poured upon man through the Incarnation, and, reaching up in return – childishly and inadequately – the love of man for God. It is a ravaged spot, yet beautiful, as the time-worn face of a woman can be beautiful if it is lit with love.

CHAPTER XVII

The Old City: II

OUTSIDE the church the evening light intensified the pallor of the flagged courtyard. A couple of Armenian monks stood talking. Their black, flowing garments and peaked hoods gave them that remote majestic appearance that characterizes the religious of the eastern churches. I went through the gateway, turned left and dropped down into the *souk* by the way I had come. A few of the shops were already lit, some by electric bulbs, others with oil lamps. In a café men sat sucking the long tubes of their *narghiles*.

A youth attached himself to me. 'Me guide you?' he said.

'I don't want a guide,' I told him.

'Me no guide,' he rejoined with engaging inconsistency. 'Me practising English.' And he thrust under my eyes an open book. On the page in front of me I read: 'Distinguish between the uses of: Push, Haul, Lug, Drag, Draw'. He came with me as far as the Seventh Station, then vanished in the crowd. I continued on my way to the Damascus Gate, then up the steps, past the money-changers and stalls arrayed with garish magazines. Outside the gate, taxi-drivers hailed me. I eluded them and, crossing the open space, began to walk north along the Nablus road. I had just passed the École Biblique when a car drew up. It was the British Consul offering me a lift.

The incident affected me strangely. The Consul's position enabled him to come and go between the two countries, but I was used to meeting him on what had now become the

'Other Side'. Here, in Jordan, he was like a being from a different planet – so remote, in a few hours, had become the country I had left that morning. A barricade, some barbed wire, a strip of waste land, was all that separated me from the other Jerusalem. My room in the American Colony looked on to buildings in Israel. Yet, Israel was more distant than Timbuctoo! I was free to travel to Timbuctoo, had I wished; but for me, as for every other visitor – unless, perhaps, some favoured diplomat – having crossed through no-man's-land, there could be no going back.

It was not only the frontier and a welter of red tape that separated the countries. In going through the Mandelbaum Gate, I had passed from one world into another: from the west into the east. And, yet, that is an over-simplification, for there is much of the east in Israel, and in Jordan more of the west than her detractors will allow for. I am thinking of the good things that the west has brought; medical knowledge, democratic ideas, a better attitude towards women. The shoddy and second rate is there, too. . . . Nevertheless, it is true to say that Israel is impatient of her eastern character: her eyes and her ambitions are set on the west. Jordan, on the other hand, lives in the tradition of her past and that is of the east. Jordan is still a country of the camel and the desert-roaming Bedouin. In Israel these have become an anachronism.

When I crossed into Jordan, I found the clocks an hour behind, for 'Summer Time' is not observed. This seemed in keeping with a general slackening of pace. In Israel there had been unceasing activity, hurry and scurry. Now, I could sit back and reflect. The things I wanted to see had been in existence a long, long time. They would still be there tomorrow.

Israel had become far away, and yet was very near.

Despite a line of partition, Jew and Arab are linked one to another like unwilling oxen harnessed to the same yoke. Try as they will, each cannot ignore, cannot forget, the other. And they try hard enough – especially the Arab who believes that the best way to be rid of something unpleasant is to behave as if it did not exist! But nostalgia and curiosity are too strong. As in Israel, for all its western character, I met Jews who looked with longing at the Old City and questioned closely each traveller who arrived from Jordan, so now I found myself asked by the Arabs: 'How is it over there? How are the Jews doing?' Or they would want to know about their own people living under Israeli rule. . . . Sometimes, bitterness was forgotten. It was not unheard of for a Jew and an Arab to exchange cigarettes over the barricade, though the next day they might be shooting at each other. The situation was a tragic one. And since then (the summer of 1955) it has become increasingly tragic, increasingly critical. . . . Yet, even tragedies have their moments of relief. In Israel they used to tell me that the mosquitoes came across from the Old City. In Jordan I was told that they were sent by the Jews. One dispassionate observer suggested that they bred in no-man's-land!

In comfort, as distinct from luxury or size, there is nothing to choose between the King David Hotel and the American Colony in Jordan. The name of the latter is misleading, for though American in origin it is less so in character than the King David, where the spacious entrance hall with swing doors, telephones ringing, page-boys calling, brought to my mind an hotel in New York. The American Colony is like a private house. Originally an Arab palace, it has vaulted ceilings, deep-set windows and strong white walls decorated with blue tiles and hanging carpets. It is built about a courtyard with a fountain and a palm tree, oleanders, and a profusion of ferns and flowers. Among the flowers are the capitals of Roman pillars and a head that for all I know might be that of Helios – or was it the Gorgon? Birds flutter and insects hum. At night there is only the splash of the fountain, and lamplight reflected on its silver spray and on a wealth of climbing geranium flinging its blossoms up to a railed balcony.

The Arab tradition in building is one of strength, simplicity and grace. Walls are solid, arches elegantly pointed, roofs domed: there is no fuss, no superfluity of decoration. This is true of new buildings as well as old – as, for example, the arcade with shops below it outside Herod's Gate or the Rockefeller Archeological Museum with its clear-cut octagonal tower, its unadorned white walls, its cloisters decorated with plaques by Eric Gill and set about a lily-pond that is hedged with lavender. The same tradition prevails in the country – in little square houses with deep-set windows and a door surmounted by a single stone. A mixture of kaolin and straw chippings covers the domed roof. I watched one of these houses being built. Poles supported the dome which was made of branches laid criss-cross with over them a rounded moulding of mud: it looked like an immense thrush's nest turned upside down.

Whether a village or Jerusalem itself, set there proud and solitary among the arid hills of Judah, the austere simplicity of the stone is appropriate to the barren rock-strewn landscape. Such a landscape is seen to advantage in the height of summer, when the violence of the sun, accentuating contours and colours, blazes down on silvery limestone and on earth ranging from a pallid terra-cotta to a red that in the shadow of a cloud darkens to purple.

In such a land, as in the hill-country of Greece or Italy, cultivation is wrested from an unwilling soil. Where all else is parched, you will see a well-tended vineyard or an olive-grove, or oxen threshing the corn. Or you will come upon a valley planted with orchards and pomegranates, then find, on its further side, the bleached bone-white wilderness.

On the slopes of the summit of a mountain, otherwise bare of trees, you will wonder to see a little grove of evergreens, dark and mysterious, consecrated far back in time to the savage rites of some Phoenician or Canaanite deity. 'Ye shall overthrow their altars,' Moses said to the Israelites, 'and break down their pillars and burn their groves with fire'.

As well as the groves, there are solitary trees, often oaks or terebinths, that have been held in veneration down the ages. They are mentioned in the stories of the prophets and the patriarchs: the trees of God, planted by himself, and not by the hand of man. The great oak tree of Abraham at Hebron is one of these.

CHAPTER XVIII

The Dome of the Rock

THE VOICE breaking upon the silence of the dawn was sad as a desert wind and cold as starlight:

Allahu akbar
Ashadan la ilaha illallah
Ashadan Mahommed rasool allah.

'God is great. There is no God but God. Mahommed is his prophet.' From the window I could see the muezzin moving round the balcony of the minaret, his figure darkly outlined against an oyster sky. Then the sky turned to gold, and the gold glittered on the heights of Nebi Samuel. From this mountain the pilgrims of old used to glimpse for the first time the walls of the Holy City. In a transport of thanksgiving they would fling themselves to the ground, praying and singing hymns. And so they gave the mountain the name *Mons Gaudii*: the Mountain of Joy. On it, too, Richard the Lion-Hearted stood, looking down upon Jerusalem that he was not granted to enter.

I went out into the golden morning. On the Nablus road men in white passed by, some walking, some on donkeys. Then women with bundles on their heads. Cocks crowed and the air was sweet with a haunting earth smell. At the Damascus Gate a carpet-seller was spreading out great blue and red rugs. As I went down the steps a little boy with a shaved head darted at me 'Ello? Ello? American?'

The shutters were opening in the *souk*: a man was arranging black and red peppers in a basket at the entrance to his shop. A woman went by, her face hidden by a black veil. Through its transparency, I could see her eyes and mouth darkly outlined. At the door of the Holy Sepulchre a turbanned Moslem smiled at me gravely. A priest was ending his Mass at the tomb: his crimson and gold vestments glowed in the candlelight. As he came out, another priest was waiting to go in – he, too, vested in crimson.

* * *

From the Holy Sepulchre and the tunnel-dark *souks*, lanes dropped down under Crusader arches to the dazzling brilliance of the Temple Court. It lay there, a vast shining plain of silvery stone set about with arcades and minarets, fountains enclosed in cages, and little domed buildings that Moslems call *qubbas*. And, among these, lest the eye be wearied by excess of light, were pines and cypresses, olives and blue-leaved acacias.

In the centre, approached on four sides by broad steps leading up under slender arches, amber yellow against the sky, stood the Dome of the Rock that is the sanctuary of the Moslems and the site of Solomon's Temple. The purple dome, topped by a golden crescent and lit with the silken sheen of its own faded gilding, was like a blossom dropped from the sky. The eight-sided building of which it formed the roof had a scarcely less ethereal quality – a delicacy that made it hard to believe it the work of human hands. From the tiles, as many-coloured and complex in pattern as the feathers in a peacock's tail, shone a blue radiance of such intensity that the sky itself seemed to take its brilliance from them. Light, too, glanced off the marble that encased the walls.

It was dark inside. I sat cross-legged on a Persian carpet,

waiting. It was all I could do, sit and wait until my eyes, dazzled by the sunlight, had accustomed themselves to the gloom.

Gradually, out of the enveloping darkness, shapes and colours revealed themselves. There were giant pillars – some square, others round – overlaid with decorations in green and white, crimson and gold. Squares and circles of red, green and blue, picked out in gold, patterned the immense ceiling. Mosaics glittered, and in the windows particles of glass flashed crimson and sapphire, lime-green and amber. It was impossible to take in the details of such splendour and richness of workmanship. As well try to fasten in the mind every blossom that makes up the glory of a herbaceous border.

A shaft of daylight came from the open door. Through a barred window I could see the staring white pavements and arcades, and in the distance the tawny slopes of the Mount of Olives. Within a few yards of where I sat two turbanned sheikhs were also sitting cross-legged on carpets. One, who was thin and bearded, was reading from the Koran on a prayer desk in front of him. He read as if he were now explaining, now arguing, his head nodding, his body swaying – he reminded me of the rabbis in the synagogues. The second sheikh was plump, with a scrubby growth on his chin, and a benevolent expression: he sat there blinking his eyes, then he stood up and waddled away into the darkness, the sleeves of his black robe flapping like a bird's wings. A young girl came in wearing a saffron-coloured dress and a shining green veil. Then a young man began to pray. He stood on one of the carpets, raised the palms of his hands, his lips moving, then he knelt, prostrated himself, touching the ground with his forehead.

Inside a Crusader grille, intricately carved, but now

overlaid with gold, sprawled an immense brown rock, *el Sakhra*, rising about seven feet above the level of the floor. From this rock, so the story goes, Mahommed ascended into heaven, mounted on his mare, *el Buraq*, which was given to him by the Archangel Gabriel. Close by, a slab of stone bears an impress of what is said to be one of the prophet's feet, while two hairs from his beard are treasured in a golden urn. In a cavity below, the spirits of the dead are reputed to meet twice a week to adore Allah. Indeed, apart from Mecca and Medina, there is nowhere on earth more sacred to the Moslems. Still more is this place sacred to the Jews. Here is all that remains of the Temple of Solomon. This rock was the threshing floor of Ornan the Jebusite, and, until the destruction of Jerusalem by the Romans, the pedestal for the altar of holocausts.

* * *

I went out into the beating sunlight. Below me in the city's eastern wall, I could see the Golden Gate – blocked long years past. Through it in 629 the Emperor Heraclius entered Jerusalem bringing with him the True Cross which he had recaptured from the Persians. It was by this gate that Jesus made his triumphal entry on Palm Sunday, riding upon the ass from Bethphage and coming down the path that is still visible on the upper slopes of Gethsemane.

To the south-east of the courtyard a flight of steps went down in gloom to what are called Solomon's Stables. This was another world, with a different, sombre splendour. Eighty-eight enormous pillars, many with holes in them through which the Crusaders are said to have tethered their horses, reached away – forming in all thirteen galleries – into what seemed an infinity of shadows. It was like a buried and long-forgotten cathedral.

CHAPTER XIX

The Mount of Olives

I

'The Mount of Olives which is before Jerusalem on the east.'

ZACHARIAH

ALEXANDER the Great, after he had taken Gaza, stood on the heights of Mount Scopus and looked down covetously upon Jerusalem. But Jaddus, the High Priest, knowing this, arrayed himself in his pontifical robes and followed by an immense crowd presented himself before the conqueror. Whereupon, the king, much moved, bowed his head and went with the priest to the Temple. . . . It was on Mount Scopus, too, that the Emperor Titus encamped his army before he beleaguered the city.

The Mount of Olives is a more southerly point on the same ridge as Scopus. But whereas the latter is associated with armies, encampment and siege, Olivet brings to mind Christ and his disciples. Here, tradition says, he taught them to pray. Here, looking down upon the city, he wept.

On the eastern spur, where the road used to run from Bethany to Jerusalem, lies the village of Bethphage, the House of Figs, to which the two disciples were sent to fetch the colt 'on which no man yet had ridden'. In the church at Bethphage there is an ancient stone, painted in faded colours, with on one side an ass and foal; on another, a crowd carrying palms in their hands; on another, Mary and

Martha prostrate at the feet of Christ and in the background Lazarus rising from the dead.

On the top of the mountain, where there is nothing to hide the heavens, nothing to dim the sparkling brilliance of the light, stands the little octagonal church of the Ascension. At a distance it looks like a thimble.

From here you see, far below, the Valley of Jehosaphat where the prophet Joel has said that God will judge mankind on the last day. Above the valley is Jerusalem, all bastioned about, and, beyond, hills and mountains, the wilderness and the Dead Sea.

II

Gethsemane lies on the lower slopes of Olivet, where it drops down to the Brook Cedron. There are, in fact, two Gethsemanes – or, rather, two parts to the same garden.

The lower of these, which belongs to the Franciscans, lies in the shadow of the church of All Nations with its flat front decorated with bright-coloured mosaics: the church fits pleasantly into a tawny landscape broken by the green of cypresses and holm oaks, junipers and firs.

The Franciscans' Gethsemane is a garden that is tended with love and care. Too much care, some will complain. Circular and star-shaped beds are packed with shrubs and flowers. Rosemary. Lavender. Jasmine. Geraniums. Asters. Dahlias. Zinnias. From among these rise twisted olive-trees, some with immense trunks that have split through age, so that the gaping wood has the appearance of hollowed rock. These olives are the soul of the garden. The word Gethsemane means an olive press, and it was most certainly to an olive grove, not a garden as we understand the word, that Jesus took himself when he wanted respite from

Jerusalem. And it was among the olive trees that he suffered his agony the night before he died.

Are these, people ask, the trees that were in the garden in the time of our lord? The Franciscans will not commit themselves. But it is reasonable to suppose that the olives we now see were born of the shoots of the trees there in Christ's day. As Pliny has said, the olive does not die: it perpetuates itself by its own shoots.

The olive is slow growing and of extraordinary longevity: for ten years it bears no fruit, nor does it reach its height of productiveness until between its fortieth and fiftieth year. Moreover, the excessive hardness of the wood – it is like a stone to touch – protects it. As to Gethsemane, it is certain that the trees have grown there for over thirteen centuries, for these olives have never been subject to the tax levied on newly planted trees since the time of the Moslem conquest.

* * *

The upper part of Gethsemane, which overhangs that of the Franciscans, is the property of the Russians. Here, on steep ground behind high walls, there is a simple grove of olives – with no attempt to adorn or improve on nature. Here, you can see what is left of the ancient pathway on which Christ trod. It leads down the hill and would have continued across the Brook, then up to the Golden Gate.

Among the trees is the convent of the Resurrection. The room in which I found myself was, in its furnishing and general atmosphere, more like an Edwardian drawing room than a convent parlour. On the walls and little tables there were photographs of the late Tzar and Tzarina, the Grand-duchesses, dignitaries of the Russian Church and members of our own Royal Family from Victorian times to the present day. Mother Mary, the Abbess, was dressed entirely in white, the other nuns in black, with the close-fitting pointed head-dress such as I had seen at Ein Kerem. Mother Mary was Scottish. She was converted to the Orthodox Church at Ein Kerem, some twenty-five years ago, at a time when she was contemplating forming an Anglican Sisterhood in Jerusalem. Her gentle face had a calm, almost mystic beauty. And this was true not only of her, but of the other nuns whom I saw in the Gethsemane convent. Their elegance of carriage, their thin figures clothed in habits reaching almost to the ground, their faces that were pale, impassive, delicate in features – their voices, clear and melodious yet seeming to rise hardly above a whisper – were the personification of a suffering aristocracy. They were out of the world now. Yet among them there were those who had seen Russia in all its glittering splendour and in the moment of its fall.

We walked up the hill, under the olive trees. The parched ground was strewn with pine needles and the air heavy with the scent of pines. Ahead of us was the church of Saint Mary Magdalen, the faded gold of its onion-shaped domes showing out of the darkness of the trees. It brought to my mind a picture I had seen of the cathedral at Kiev.

'It is fitting that the gold be faded on our domes,' Mother Mary said to me. 'Ours is a church in exile.'

Unlike the Orthodox Russians in Israel, who have come to terms with the Communistic regime, these of whom I write will have no compromise, choosing, rather, to wait with patience for the day of deliverance, according to God's will, in God's time.

Inside the church there was the same faded but uncompromising dignity. It was the hour of Vespers. The voices of the nuns had a melancholy loveliness, and their faces – some of them young – showed white in the flickering light of tapers. A bearded priest gorgeously vested appeared from behind the screen that hides the altar, then disappeared. Incense rose in clouds. Lights burned before ikons: the rain-bringing Arab ikon of the Blessed Virgin Hodegistria and the ikon of Our Lady of Egorer which was rescued from the bombing of Kiev.

In the crypt lies the body of a grand-daughter of Queen Victoria, the Grand-Duchess Elizabeth, who, at the foundation of this church by the Emperor Alexander III in 1888, expressed the wish that she might be buried here. Little did she know how this would come to be. In 1917 she was murdered with the Tzar and his family. Her body which had been flung into a pit along with that of her attendant, Sister Barbara, was smuggled by a monk to Harbin, in China, from where it was brought to the Holy Land on board a British battleship.

I came away from these nuns sad for their sadness, yet happy for their steadfast patience and for a peace that outshone their sufferings. The sufferings of the Russian nuns in Jerusalem have indeed been intense. After General Allenby's deliverance of the city, some of them were found breaking stones by the wayside, so great was their poverty.

CHAPTER XX

The Via Dolorosa

'Now from the sixth hour there was darkness over all the land unto the ninth hour'. SAINT MATTHEW

THE Fortress Antonia looks down upon the Temple Court. For this reason, Josephus explained, Roman legionaries were stationed in the fortress during important feasts, to suppress any attempt at insurrection by the Jews, 'the Temple being the watch-tower of the city as the Antonia was of the Temple'.

The Antonia was the Praetorium of the Gospels, where, in preference to Herod's Palace on Mount Zion, Pontius Pilate took up residence during the Passover. Here he questioned Christ, and having questioned him, went into the courtyard that was called Lithostrotos, the paved place, and said to the Jews – 'I find no fault in this man'. But they, crying out the more, shouted: 'Away with him, crucify him'. And Jesus, carrying his cross, went out to a place called 'the place of a skull, which is called in Hebrew Golgotha'.

Christopher Smart, that gentle, tortured poet, lover of God and his creatures, wrote that the glory of God 'is always in the east, but cannot be seen for the Cloud of the Crucifixion'.

The cloud of the Crucifixion still hangs upon Jerusalem: the darkness that was over the earth.

The sun shines, yet the Via Dolorosa is dark. Walls with barred windows and iron lamp-brackets rise steep on either side. Arches fling clear-cut shadows. Buried deep under the pavement is the way that Christ trod. Under it, too, in the crypt of the Convent of Notre Dame de Zion, is the Lithostrotos with its huge flagged stones cut into grooves to prevent horses from slipping. Also cut into the stones are symbols that were used by Roman soldiers in a game called *Basilicus*, the King. The letter B recurs. There is a line cut by a sword and a crown put together of thorns. They chose a king in make-believe, heaped honours on him, bade him satisfy his slightest whim, then, the farce ended, put him to death. That was the game; but sometimes they left the world of fantasy, choosing for their king a condemned prisoner.

It is Friday. In the heat of the afternoon a crowd, following a few Franciscans, straggles from one Station of the Cross to the next. Here, Jesus was condemned to die. Here, he received his cross. Here he fell. . . . Onlookers watch from doorways with the indifferent expression of those to whom a sight is long familiar – as familiar as once was the sight of a prisoner led by the Roman legionaries to die on a gibbet. Others stare in curiosity. A young man with dark glasses takes his stand on a flight of steps. A camera snaps. A woman's clipped voice says; 'My dear, what's this in aid of?'

The crowd, joined by newcomers, straggles on, then kneels at the place where Christ was met by his Mother. The priest who leads the prayers has been overtaken by his followers: they wait while he pushes his way through.

The Via Dolorosa crosses the street that runs to the Damascus Gate. At the corner a woman sitting on the pavement weighs peppers in a pair of scales. Another has eggs for sale in a round flat basket. On the floor of a shop rabbits are nibbling leaves and a fowl clucks in a coop.

'They compelled Simon of Cyrene to carry his cross.' The

way is uphill now. The sun beats down. The crowd begins to flag.

At the Sixth Station a door stands open into the chapel of the Sisters of Charles du Foucauld. On the austere altar candles burn in a black, seven-branched candlestick, their light reflected in the crimson and blue of low, arched windows.

In the darkness of the *souk* we stop at the Seventh Station that has become my landmark in Jerusalem's tortuous streets. From here I can find my way north to the Damascus Gate, or south, with a turn or two, to the Holy Sepulchre. To the east, dark lanes drop down to the Temple. Francis Street goes westward, up wide low steps.

We go uphill, up Francis Street, to where a cross with the word *Nika* in Greek lettering is cut into a wall. 'Weep not for me, but for yourselves and your children,' he said to the women of Jerusalem.

The convent of Saint Charalampos blocks the way. We begin to retrace our steps to the *souk*. As we go down a man leading a donkey laden with sacks is coming up. So is a porter burdened with crates. The donkey-man and the porter are wrangling, first between themselves, then with the crowd. Angry voices rise. We cannot go down. They cannot come up. The crowd mutters and surges. I feel myself thrust against a wall. There is a smell of garlic and sweat. Again the *souk*. Then up to an open space in front of the church of the Copts. Calvary is near. The apse of the Holy Sepulchre is in sight, and the roof of Saint Helena's church built above the place where the Cross was found.

In the church of the Holy Sepulchre flickering tapers lighten the darkness that goes up to Calvary. The Son of Man is stripped of his garments and nailed upon the Tree. Here his mother stood, and here Saint John.

The voice of the Franciscan rises like a lament, praying away sorrow:

Pater noster qui es in caelis. . . .

The crowd picks it up:

Panem nostrum quotidianum. . . .

Down again in darkness, past the Stone of Anointing, to the Tomb. The last prayers are said. The way of sorrow is ended. In the Tomb a light shines. The Star that is set will rise again, never more to set, for, 'the setting has believed in the rising, and that is the new creation.'

CHAPTER XXI

Copts, Ethiopians and Armenians

I

I WOULD like to know more about the Copts.

They came to Jerusalem from Egypt, not later, it would seem, than the fifteenth century – probably under the Mamelukes. Their name is a corruption of the Greek word for Egypt, and their language the tongue of the ancient Egyptians.

Neither rich nor powerful, they have held their ground in the Holy Sepulchre with steadfastness and in the face of opposition. Their altar, which backs on to the marble structure enclosing the Tomb of Christ, is enclosed in an iron-wrought grille. Whenever I stopped to look at it, I was filled with that sense of wonder that I felt as a child when I gazed at a decorated Christmas tree or into a toy-shop window. There were tapers and silver lamps, little ikons glittering with gold, and a large silver ikon brought from Egypt, of Mary with the Holy Child. In the middle of all this was an alarm clock with a loud comfortable tick. A priest wearing black robes and a small deep-blue turban kept watch. Whenever I turned away from the altar, it seemed to me that his dark eyes smiled. But it was a smile so elusive that sometimes I wondered whether it was there at all. When I lit a taper he sprinkled my hand with scent as is the custom of the Copts, symbolizing the gratitude of Christ's mother.

A Bedouin girl.

Bethlehem: the head-dress introduced by the Crusaders

The *siq* through which one rides to Petra

The Coptic Patriarchal Church is scarcely a hundred yards from the Holy Sepulchre. In it candles burn before a painting of Mary with the child in her arms. For it was here, at the back of the church, during Vespers on the evening of July the twenty-fifth, nineteen hundred and fifty-four, that a multitude of persons, Moslems as well as Christians of different churches, claimed to have seen the mother of Christ moving among the congregation. So overcome was the priest, that though a tough strong man as he himself said, he could not continue the service. This was a second apparition. The first was a week earlier at eleven o'clock in the morning in the Coptic School of Saint Anthony of Egypt, almost adjoining the church. Primary Class Five was having Religious Instruction – Moslems among them – when the children began to shout '*El Adra! El Adra!*' ('the Virgin!'). She was there, they declared, in the window across the courtyard.

Consternation followed and the school secretary was summoned. He quietened the children, and locked the door. Soon they were crying out again. This time the vision was in their own room, which is now a blue-walled chapel decorated with an ikon. A plaque outside the window records what happened.

All this is set forth in the Coptic Patriarchal Journal. Yet the Copts have shown no inordinate pride, as though thinking themselves favoured beyond others. 'She did not come for our sakes,' their bishop said. 'She came because this place is holy, being within a few yards of Calvary and the Tomb.'

II

Monks of the Ethiopian church once had their place in the Holy Sepulchre. For the past hundred years, however, they have lived on the roof, above the church of Saint Helena, in huts that look like an African village. When I was in the Israel quarter of Jerusalem I had visited their round, domed church in Abyssinia Street, which is off the Street of the Prophets. Great dark-skinned men had greeted me with salaams and murmurs of approbation on hearing that shortly I would be seeing their brothers on the 'Other Side'.

Abyssinian, or Ethiopian, Christianity is in the main Coptic: both are monophysite, which means that they do not distinguish the divine and human natures of Christ as laid down by the Council of Chalcedon in the year 451. Legend has attributed the beginning of the Ethiopian church to Saint Matthew and Saint Bartholomew, as well as to Philip's conversation with the eunuch who was an officer in the service of Candace, Queen of Ethiopia. Historically, the church goes back to the fourth century. Frumentius, a Phoenician captive, who became tutor to the royal family, is related to have converted his charges. He then went to Alexandria where the Patriarch made him the first Ethiopian bishop or *Abuna* – the word means father and is associated with the Aramaic *Abba*. From that time, apart from certain interruptions, the head of the Ethiopian church was a Copt appointed by the Patriarch of Cairo. In the year 1950, however, the Emperor Haile Selassie enacted that one of his own people should hold the position.

There are links between the Abyssinians and the Jews. The old name of Ethiopia was Cosh, and Cosh was a grandson of Noah. There is, too, a tradition that the Ark of the Covenant is hidden somewhere in Ethiopia and that for this reason the land is especially favoured of God. One of the titles of the Emperor is the Conquering Lion of the

Tribe of Judah, for the Golden Lion of Judah is the symbol of the royal family which claims descent from Menelik the first, the son of Solomon and the Queen of Sheba. An ikon in Cairo shows the family tree as taking root from this union. Ethiopians sometimes describe themselves as a Sabaean people, and Saba is another form of Sheba. They call the Red Sea the Sabaean Sea.

Perhaps because of their association with the Jews, the Ethiopians keep the Sabbath as well as Sunday. They also distinguish between food that is clean and unclean, refusing to eat the flesh of animals that do not chew the cud or have cloven hoofs.

Their liturgical language is Ge'ez, an ancient tongue of Sabaean origin known only to the more educated of the clergy and a handful of scholars. Their calendar, too, is strange by western standards: Christmas is celebrated once a month, and I am told that Pontius Pilate is included among their saints. Confession is the rule of the church, but sometimes it takes an unusual form. A man meeting a priest will call out 'Absolve me' and the priest answer, 'Be absolved'. Sometimes absolution includes a blow over the shoulder with a branch of the Woira tree as a sign of deliverance from Satan's power.

Umbrellas are a mark of distinction in Abyssinia and consequently much used in ceremonial. Some are red, others made of cloth of gold. They are often embroidered with silver crosses or figures of the saints. Occasionally the fringe is hung with bells. The priests engage in ritual dances accompanied by drums ornamented with silver and beaten with the palm of the hand. They also use a rattle made of wood and brass and closely resembling the *sistrum* employed in the ancient worship of Egyptian Isis. This instrument, which is said to take seven years to learn to play, makes a shrill, shivering sound. The legend is that it was introduced in its present form by an Abyssinian saint called Yarad who was reminded of the Trinity by the sounds of three birds singing in a tree.

Late on the night that follows Holy Saturday the monks on the roof of the Holy Sepulchre celebrate a rite known as Searching for the Body of Christ. They go round the roof in the light of the moon, chanting in weird melancholy tones, beating their drums and shaking the *sistrum*. So, lamenting the Saviour they cannot find, they await the dawn.

III

Close to the Garden of Gethsemane forty-six wide low steps go down into the darkness of the underground Crusader Church known as the Tomb of the Virgin.

At either end of each step a candle was burning, whether as votive offerings or to light the way. From out of the darkness came the voices of the Armenians: beautiful, poignant.... The music of the Armenians, both religious and secular (the two are inseparable), is born of their suffering. No people, unless it be the Jews, have suffered more than the Armenians, through massacre, exile, deportation, oppression, devastation of their land, destruction of their homes. A medieval pilgrim to Jerusalem remarked on the beauty of the Armenian women and men. I, too, saw beautiful Armenians. But more striking than their beauty is a look of suffering on their faces: not so much personal suffering as an inherited racial agony carried down from one generation to the next.

The ancient home of the Armenians, from which they have been scattered over the earth, is a plateau bordered on the north by part of the Black Sea, reaching eastward almost to the Caspian Sea and to the south merging into the plains of Mesopotamia. Here, tradition says, was the original home of the human race. Here, the Tigris and the Euphrates and the Araxes have their sources. Here, the great volcanic cone of Mount Ararat rises from a barren plain. On Ararat it is said the Ark rested, and there are those who say that it is there today, on the summit of the mountain. Ararat pointing to the sky has been at all times an inspiration to the people of Armenia: its cone-shaped top is said to be symbolized in their architecture and in the peaked cowls of the clergy.

The Armenian church of Saint James the Great is one of the most beautiful in Jerusalem. It is decorated with tiles and pictures, splendid carpets and woodwork that is inlaid with mother-of-pearl and ivory. The shrine dedicated to the apostle is entered through a door adorned with tortoiseshell and nacre. In the porch there are gongs made of brass and wood that are a reminder of the treaty between the Christians and Moslems in the year 637 when the ringing of church bells was forbidden. Gongs, however, were allowed in consequence of a Moslem legend that Noah used a gong to summon the workmen who were building the Ark.

Armenians sometimes remove their shoes before entering a church. In the church, they either stand or sit on a carpet. They confess their sins publicly, the priest reading out a list of offences and each person concerned nodding assent. At the end of Mass, which is celebrated with great dignity and ceremonial, it is customary to distribute blessed bread to the congregation.

Chateaubriand, in recording his visit to Jerusalem, related that he was entertained by the Armenian Patriarch whom he found wearing garments of silk and seated on a cushion, like a wealthy Turk. Coffee and sweetmeats and clean napkins were brought. Aloe wood was burning and the perfume of essence of roses was so strong as to be almost overwhelming.

The present Armenian Patriarch is a poet of considerable distinction.

CHAPTER XXII

Bethlehem

I

I made me gardens and orchards, and I planted trees in them of all kinds of fruits:
I made me pools of water, to water therewith the wood that bringeth forth trees. ECCLESIASTES

WE STOOD – Stewart Perowne, the Poetical Banker and myself – looking down through the trees at the Pools of Solomon. They were like three immense sinks made of stone, one at a slightly lower level than the other, drained dry by a year of exceptional drought.

Then we continued on our way to Bethlehem.

At first we walked three abreast. But presently we dropped into single file, partly because the way was narrow and strewn with stones, partly because the quiet of the evening made conversation an intrusion. Stewart Perowne was in front, his *keffiyeh* worn at a rakish angle, and his trousers the colour of geraniums. Behind him was the Poetical Banker. Anyone less like a banker I have never seen. He might have been an actor, or a musician or a poet. Not a banker. His bank, moreover, was as unexpected as himself. It was in the Via Dolorosa, on the first floor of a building called the Desmoterion Christi, the prison of Christ, that belongs to the Orthodox Greeks. There is a dungeon in it, and chapels. Bearded clergy pass in the shadows.

I came last. My attention was distracted by the squills

which I had not seen before. They shot up pale and slender from the rocky soil, their tiny mauve blossoms just beginning to open on the greyish green stems. There is something unreal about these plants. They seem, like the asphodel, to belong to another world. Noah is said to have taken them into the Ark to feed the gazelles.

We were following the aqueduct built by Pontius Pilate. Beginning south of Solomon's Pools, it winds round the hills, passes under the Pools, then goes on to Bethlehem. From there it again skirts the hills, and ends in the Temple Court at Jerusalem. Pilate built it with money from the Carbona, the sacred treasury, in consequence of which he angered the Jews, was summoned to Rome, and reprimanded by the Emperor Tiberius.

Far below, to the east, the village of Urtas with its convent of the Hortus Conclusus (the words *Urtas* and *Hortus* are one), lay upon the slopes of the valley. 'I have built my beloved a garden,' said the writer of the Canticle. The garden, is a symbol of the soul that is in communion with God. 'And their soul shall be as a watered garden: and they shall not sorrow any more.' It was a gracious spot of running streams, orchards and olive groves, figs and pomegranates, and neat vineyards each with a little stone tower. 'They made me the keeper of the vineyards.' And again: 'There was a certain householder which planted a vineyard and hedged it round about and digged a winepress in it and built a tower and let it out to husbandmen'.

Urtas, it is said, was the garden of which Solomon sings: his paradise rich in noble fruits, henna and spikenard, saffron, calamus, and cinnamon, myrrh and aloes and incense-bearing trees. Its green luxuriance is the more lovely because the surrounding landscape is treeless and barren. Yet this, too, has an austere beauty. The evening light accentuated the red of the soil and the staring white of limestone rock. Limestone has a quality all its own, in that it not only reflects light but holds it on into the dusk and darkness.

Away across the valley I saw the Herodium: a fierce and not unfitting reminder of that grim unhappy king who in his last illness gave orders that the leading men among the Jews be killed to ensure that his death might be attended by universal mourning. It seemed to symbolize, too, the terror of the wilderness that on its farther side dropped down to the Dead Sea.

This wilderness is rich in memories of David. It was when fighting here that he was overcome with a longing for a drink from the well of Bethlehem, then in possession of the Philistines. 'Oh that one would give me to drink of the water from the well of Bethlehem which is by the gate,' he cried. Whereupon three of his men broke through the host of the enemy, drew water from the well and brought it to David. But the king, ashamed to think at what hazard it had been brought, would not drink. And taking the water, he poured it out to the Lord.

II

'*And thou, Bethlehem Ephratah, though thou be little among the thousands of Judah, yet out of thee shall he come forth unto me that is to be ruler in Israel; whose goings forth have been from of old, from everlasting.*' MICAH

The town hung there, above fields enclosed in stone walls. It was silvery white, its flat-roofed houses terraced one above the other, with towers and belfries rising from among them, and here and there clusters of cypress trees.

We lost sight of it as the path bent round past a grove

of olives. The hollow trunks of some were filled with stones, and under each the earth was banked. Then we saw the town again. It became yet more white as the twilight deepened. It seemed to breathe peace, like a stone-built English village, seen in the half-light of a summer evening.

Jerusalem is fierce: a city often beleaguered. Time and again the church of the Holy Sepulchre has suffered destruction by fire and sword. In comparison, the history of Bethlehem is uneventful. When the Persians laid waste the cities of the Roman empire, burnt Jerusalem and imprisoned the Patriarch, they spared the church of the Nativity at Bethlehem, for, seeing in it a picture of the Magi bringing their gifts to the Christ Child, they were filled with wonder, 'nor was their respect and affection for their ancestors less than if they had been alive'.

The path dropped down. Below, to the right, was a well. Was it from that well they had taken the water to David? Women with pitchers were gathered about it. One of them wore the tall white head-dress inherited from Crusader times. We began to climb the hill that leads into the centre of the town. A flock of sheep was coming towards us, their hooves pattering.

III

'*Ecce, in hoc parvo terrae foramine caelorum conditor natus est.*'
SAINT PAULA, writing on the Cave of the Nativity.

It was early morning. I bowed my head to enter the low doorway into the church of the Nativity. Inside, it was cool and large and empty, like one of the great basilicas at Rome. There is a royal splendour about this church built where a King was born. In it, too, in 1101 a king was crowned: Baldwin I, who refused to be crowned in Jerusalem, thinking it unfitting to be thus honoured in a city where his Lord had worn a crown of thorns. . . . Shafts of light coming through windows set high in the walls broke upon faded mosaics and huge golden-red pillars.

At first I did not see the paintings on the pillars. Then one by one mitres and halos took shape; crimson cloaks and purple tunics, calm stylized faces, and a Virgin holding a Child.

Lamps hidden in striped cotton bags hung from the ceiling, with a ball under each. The balls were large and bright: red and blue, lime-green and gold and silver.

'How gaudy those balls look,' a woman's voice said at my elbow. Her words rasped in the stillness of the church.

'I think they are charming,' I said crossly. 'Not at all inappropriate in a church that honours a child.'

* * *

On either side of the high altar a flight of worn rounded steps led down into the cave where Christ was born. It was dark, and yet full of light. Tapers were burning, and the glow of lamps was reflected on a silver star nailed into the floor and bearing upon it the words:

'*Hic de Virgine Maria Jesus Christus natus est.*' Above the star there was an altar, and in the nitch behind it an ancient mosaic, damaged, yet still showing Mary in robes of silver and blue and amethyst, and the face of the ox looking towards the manger.

A few yards away, on the far side of the cave, three steps between pillars – one red and strong, the other white and delicately carved into a spiral – went down into the chapel of the Manger. The Manger today is a rock-shelf overlaid with marble. In the church of Constantine it had a covering of silver. Saint Jerome regretted this. 'In honouring Christ,' he wrote, 'we have taken away that clay manger and put in its place a silver one. I prize more the one that has been taken away.'

I knelt on the pavement of the tiny chapel, while a Franciscan said Mass at the altar dedicated to the Magi. Across the cave the lamplight flickered on the silver star. There was no one but the priest and the server. No sound but the murmur of the Latin:

> '*Et ecce, stella, quam viderant in Oriente, antecedebat eos usque dum veniens staret supra ubi erat puer. Videntes autem stellam, gavisi sunt gaudio magno valde. Et intrantes domum invenerunt puerun cum Maria matre eius.*'

The star filled my thoughts. Was it, as some supposed, the conjunction of Jupiter and Saturn in the year 6 B.C.? Or the providential appearance of a comet? Or, as Saint Augustine said, was it a new star, unlike those that had observed their appointed course since the beginning of time, shining forth at the wonder of a virgin bearing a child? '*Novo partu virginis novum sidus apparuit.*' And was it seen by the Magi, as some held, two years before the birth of Christ? Or did it appear, as others believed, on the night he was born, and the Magi travelled in such hot haste that, whether by divine aid or by the speed of their camels, they completed their journey in thirteen days? . . . The silver star on the floor. The star that shone over Bethlehem. The Magi. The shepherds. The angels. The ox and the ass. Joseph. Mary. The Child. They were all gathered into the Mass that was being offered on the altar.

* * *

A Franciscan brother was sweeping the floor in front of the altar of the Magi. A Greek monk was also sweeping near the place of the star. Close by an Armenian was filling a lamp. Much has been written about the squabbles at Bethlehem between the different churches. The Greeks, the Armenians, the Latins, have their allotted ground, their number of lamps, their rights and privileges. No one would pretend there have not been quarrels, some serious, none of them edifying. Yet, now, the atmosphere is more peaceful than for many years. A Franciscan told me a story that I like to remember. A Greek monk, hoping to extend the space allotted to his church, shifted his carpet a little further each day in the direction of the Latin altar. Seeing this, a Franciscan brought a pair of scissors and snipped off some inches of the offending carpet. I heard this story again from a Greek. This time the roles were reversed.

* * *

I went out of the cave by an underground passage that leads up to the church of Saint Catherine of Alexandria. It is tunnelled out of the natural rock, and off it are caverns that have been made into chapels. The first, which is dedicated to Saint Joseph, contains a painting on copper of the Saint being warned by an angel in a dream to flee with the child and his mother into Egypt. From here steps go down into the chapel of the Holy Innocents, those first martyrs whom Prudentius likened to rose-buds scattered by the wind:

Quos lucis ipso in limine
Christi insecutor sustulit
Ceu turbo nascentes rosas.

Another of the chapels is said to be the cell in which Saint Jerome finished his translation of the Scriptures. In another is buried his pupil, Saint Eusebius of Cremona; in another Saint Paula, with her daughter, Eustochium. Saint Jerome wrote many letters to Paula, who was a Roman widow, descended from the family of the Scipios. She founded a convent at Bethlehem, as well as the monastery of which Saint Jerome was superior.

The winding, taper-lit passage and the little rough-hewn cells, one opening into another, with their lights and pictures, were like a symbol of the overflowing of the Incarnation into the world beyond.

CHAPTER XXIII

Refugees at Jericho

I

BETHANY, the home of Mary and Martha, sits upon one of the eastern spurs of the Mount of Olives. It is a white, dusty village with narrow lanes and sharp turnings. Figs and almonds grow in little fields enclosed by loose stone walls: olives and carob trees shoot up from among broken Crusader masonry. In the year 1143, Melisende, Queen of Jerusalem, bought Bethany from the custodians of the Holy Sepulchre and built a convent there. One of its early abbesses was the queen's youngest sister, Joveta, who had spent a year of her childhood as a hostage among the Moslems and later became a nun at Saint Anne's in Jerusalem.

Eusebius saw the tomb of Lazarus at Bethany. It is still shown today, up a steep lane littered with stones. Children selling postcards gathered round me at its entrance, then a wizened old man holding a lighted taper went ahead of me down steps, into darkness. There was a vestibule and an inner chamber, cut into the chalky rock, where the body would have been laid.

Two parties from England filled the confined space. Each was led by a clergyman – one wearing a Balliol blazer, the other a cream alpaca coat. Suddenly they were aware of each other.

'Hello, old boy!' boomed the one in the blazer, clapping his hand on the other's shoulder.

'My dear fellow!' replied his friend in the alpaca coat.

II

'*The wilderness that goeth up from Jericho.*' JOSHUA

From Bethany the road to Jericho drops with abrupt turns into the Wadi el-Haud at the head of which there is a spring known as the Fountain of the Apostles. Its water is clear and sparkling, yet reputed to be dangerous to drink by reason of innumerable leeches. Further along this road is the Khan Hadur, more generally known as the Inn of the Good Samaritan, with above it the ruins of the Crusader Castle of Blood. Saint Jerome wrote of the Mountain of Blood 'in the country of Judah and Benjamin which drops down from Jerusalem to Jericho'. The hills, here, are stained with red. All are devoid of vegetation and their slopes strangely creased and folded so as to resemble giant sand-dunes.

The road we followed was black and smooth. But presently we turned off, taking the ancient Roman track which Christ and his disciples would have used. It was strewn with stones, and clouds of dust rose in front of the car. The mountains pressed in on every side, grim against a glaring sky. The silence was terrifying. From high ground that sloped up from the road there was a view across a valley to the monastery of Saint George. Its blue domes looked absurdly gay in this scene of desolation. Apart from the domes, the building was sand-coloured, like the wall of mountain that reached above it and below. Indeed, it might have been carved out of the rock, not built upon it.

A little distance from the monastery there was an aqueduct, its water falling in a thin silver cascade. The flow of the water was cool and lovely among the parched mountains: the sound came across the valley like the tinkle of bells.

The road dropped in hair-pin bends. The heat was stifling. We were below the level of the sea, and still we went down. Suddenly, spread below was the plain of Jericho. Jericho renowned for balsam. The City of the Moon. The City of Palms. It was green with palms and banana groves and orange trees. Beyond, was the turquoise daub of the Dead Sea with the mountains of Moab on the far side.

* * *

There are three Jerichos.

Modern Jericho has a long street that opens into a square with a fountain. There are villas, shops, cafés, a couple of hotels and a cinema.

Jericho of the New Testament is represented by a mound where was once the palace of Herod the Great. Herod, who died at Jericho, spent a fortune on the place. As well as his own luxurious winter residence, he built a hippodrome and an amphitheatre and laid out gardens watered by aqueducts. The town was a present to him from Cleopatra, who had received it from Mark Antony. It was here, too, that the publican Zacchaeus scrambled into the sycamore tree to see Jesus pass. Antonine of Picenza was shown this tree enclosed in a roofless oratory.

Then there is Old Testament Jericho: the Canaanite city round whose walls the Israelites carried the Ark of the Covenant for seven days, and on the seventh day they carried it round seven times and at the trumpet call of Joshua the walls fell. This Jericho was the school of the prophets: Elijah lived here, and Elisha, his disciple. I stood on the dusty mound above the excavations. Below was the Fountain of Elisha. Women went up and down, their veils like gay flowers – red and pink, purple and saffron. They carried pitchers on their heads; those that were full standing upright, the empty ones resting on their side. The sun beat down. The ground under my feet was like burning coals. Bee-eaters flew round and round, darting and dipping, flashing turquoise and gold. The Mount of the Temptation was black against a brassy sky.

The well. The women passing up and down. The sun and the scorching earth. The birds, dipping and darting. The mountain against the sky. That was all. And yet it was not. There was something more: an influence, brooding, oppressive, that not even the bright whirring birds could dispel. It was the influence of the Jericho that goes back to a past far beyond Elisha, Elijah or Joshua: immortalized in the finds of the archaeologists – shell eyes that stare out of faces of unbaked clay and amphorae, that grin and leer and mock. It was as though they were staring at me now, as I stood on the mound in the stupifying heat. They were not mere memories of exhibits seen in a museum; they went back into my past, were one with the African fetish masks that in my childhood had looked down by day from the walls of the red distempered hall, and at night made the darkness of the nursery horrible.

III

The Arab refugee camp was on the plain, at the foot of the mountains. There were huts as far as the eye could see, and white glaring dust.

We were taken first – two American journalists, a French journalist and myself – to the Camp Officer. He sat at a desk in a white, sparsely furnished room, answering, as best he could, the questions put to him by the Americans. His plump, highly coloured face crinkled anxiously. Though he spoke English adequately, it was plain that he did not always understand what was being said to him. He looked like a worried child. The telephone kept ringing, the door opening and shutting. An Arab came in; tall, in spotless white, bearing himself with dignity. Then another who had weak eyes and a distracted expression: he talked wildly. Then a nurse. Then a policeman who grinned at us and settled himself on a chair. Lemon drinks were brought, and little cups of black coffee.

We went out into the grilling heat. Except for a few mimosa saplings near the Camp Officer's hut there was not a tree, not a vestige of shade. Only the sun and the glaring dust. We were visitors for an hour or so. The refugees had been there for seven years. They might be there another seven. Who could tell? And, in high places, who cared? Some had died from exposure to heat, some from the winter cold.

We walked across to the girls' section. Some of them were standing at a long table, cleaning dates, others cooking them in an aluminium cauldron. They wore brightly coloured dresses. Rose and saffron, violet and green. Many had bracelets and rings. They eyed us, then made remarks to one another. A few smiled. In another room younger girls were embroidering: designs in red and black or green and black on white linen. They came up and stood round us, holding out their work – some eagerly, some with reluctance. '*Bien, très bien,*' murmured the French journalist taking a piece of embroidery into his hand. Dark eyes smiled. A few stared insolently.

We walked on in the dust and under the beating sun, in the direction of the medical section. Suddenly I was aware of a great crowd, made up mostly of women, moving towards us surging this way and that. They were shouting and gesticulating.

'Wait here a minute,' the Camp Officer said. But the crowd had already borne down on us. Their voices were shrill. The officer spoke to them calmly, repeating the same words again and again reassuringly, as one might speak to frightened children. His face had crinkled with concern.

'They are so emotional,' he said, shaking his head as he turned away.

'But what has happened?' I asked.

'A child! She fell into a cauldron of potatoes while the dinner was being given out . . . I don't think she is badly hurt. She's with the doctor.' As he spoke two women broke away from the rest and came up to me face to face. They were talking excitedly and wringing their hands, and their eyes, that looked into mine, were sullen with despair. One of them laid her hand on my wrist and I put my hand on hers.

'What is it, what does she say?' I asked the officer.

His face crinkled again.

'She says, "Take us away from here".'

We went into the medical hut. The child who had fallen into the cauldron was there. She stood naked on a bed while the doctor put cotton wool over her burns. Her olive-coloured body was shiny; it looked as if it were covered with oil, and her feet were treading up and down. She made a strange, high-pitched moaning sound, like a little animal. The doctor spoke to her soothingly. 'She is not badly hurt,' a nurse said. 'It is the shock.'

'It must be difficult for you,' I said to the Camp Officer as we walked away.

'By God, it is,' he answered with sudden fierceness. 'You have to tell them everything again and again and again. . . . The only thing they want is to go back to their lands.'

'Could they not be given other lands?' One of the Americans asked.

'To go to other lands would be to settle . . . it would mean permanency. That is a situation they won't accept. When we tried planting trees, some of the refugees tore them up. A tree is permanent. . . . They want the lands that have been taken from them – their homes. At least we have achieved something in getting them into houses, and out of tents.'

I appreciated his last remark. I had seen the camp outside Bethlehem: the awful squalor of tents, one almost on top of the other.

'Have any of the refugees work outside the camp?' the American went on.

'A few have.'

'And the pay? Are they well paid?'

'Not very. . . . And they have no future, nothing to look forward to.'

In another hut a doctor was attending to a queue of male patients. I sat on a bed, watching. He was a fat man wearing an open shirt and blue cotton trousers that were tight across his stomach. His voice was kind. The patients were in striped pyjamas. Some of them were suffering from trachoma. Their eyes were bloodshot and the lids swollen. One man, who was blind, felt his way with his hands, pathetically.

The doctor came over to us.

'Is there anything you would like to ask?' he said.

'How does health compare with Mandate times?' said the Frenchman.

'As to actual diseases, much the same. But these people suffer from prolonged undernourishment and lack of vitamins – from all the evils that come from inadequate food and overcrowding.'

'I guess some of the trouble is psychological,' one of the Americans broke in.

'Indeed yes. We have more cases of neuroses than in the old days. Especially among adults and older children. They miss their homes. They have no security, no purpose. Children born here suffer less, because they have known no other life.'

I asked if there was any psychological treatment.

'Unfortunately, no. It is more than we can do to attend to their bodily needs. We prescribe vitamins and order supplementary rations, but nothing makes up for the loss of their homes. Vitamins and rations don't cure worry.'

In a near-by hut mothers with young children were waiting for supplementary rations. Women in overalls handed out bowls of soup. Some of the mothers were beautiful. But they had strained anxious faces that made them look old before their time. One had a haunted expression which I remember to this day. More women and children gathered about me as we went out. The Americans wanted to take pictures, but were asked not to.

We were shown two houses, built of concrete.

The first was for a man, his wife and five children. It consisted of one room with an oil stove and bedding rolled up in a corner. The walls were bare except for newspaper cuttings of cinema stars. A kitten slept on a window-ledge: I wondered how this came to be, for we were told that the refugees were not allowed to keep pets. Flies buzzed, but the building was not dirty. The occupier wore jeans and a black trilby. His expression was desperate. 'We go mad if something be not done,' he said, snapping his fingers.

The second house belonged to a woman who was able to earn some money as a midwife. There was an attempt at a garden; a rosemary bush, and a few marigolds in a bed surrounded by jam-jars.

We walked back to the car, passing on the way women with children in their arms, and men standing dejectedly in groups or sitting in doorways. Some little boys had attached themselves to us. They stood there watching us drive away. A couple of them waved. The sun beat down on a desert of white dust.

IV

From Jericho we went to Beit-safafa, a frontier village between Jerusalem and Bethlehem.

Permits had to be obtained at an UNWRA headquarters near Bethlehem, where we were interviewed by men in uniform. They gave us lemon tea while they telephoned to the police at Jerusalem. The room in which we sat was piled high with sacks of flour and barrels of dried milk.

We set off in a jeep. It rattled over stony ground until we came to a police post, where they had already been informed of our arrival. A policeman came up to the car, called out our names from a paper and asked the nationality of each. Another was standing on the roof of the building, holding binoculars to his eyes. Then a third came up and got into the jeep. He carried a rifle, and a cartridge-belt was slung over his shoulder. As soon as we reached the village, we were met by yet another policeman, also armed.

Before we set foot on the ground a crowd had gathered about us. There were women and children among them. The men soon shooed these away, allowing only a couple of older boys to remain. All listened in respectful silence when an old man who looked like a Bible patriarch began to speak. He had parched skin and dark faded eyes. His blue tunic was carefully patched with material of a lighter shade. The policeman interpreted what he said, but much of it was easy to follow, for he spoke not simply with his lips, but with his face and his hands. His son, he explained, was across the barrier; he had been there when the division was made, living on property that belonged to the family. He himself happened to be on this side. He had been forbidden to go back to his home, nor was communication permitted. He was living now in the house of another, cut off from his son and their land. As he spoke, we were standing at the barrier of barbed wire. It ran down the middle of the street. On this side was Jordan, on the other Israel. So much for a truce line drawn on a map at a conference table on the Island of Rhodes!

Then an elderly man with round puffy cheeks told us how at the time of the truce his daughter was in hospital on the 'Other Side'. She had not been allowed to return nor could he go across to her. He told us, too, of a wedding between a couple who were betrothed before the outbreak of the fighting. After a delay of eight months a permit was granted to the girl to go through the Mandelbaum Gate to join her future husband in Israel. A wedding party was held on both sides of the barbed wire.

Another man pointed to land enclosed by a stone wall. 'My fields,' he said, shrugging his shoulders, 'and another cultivates them!'

Our visit was something of an event for the village. Women and children stared from doorways or from the roofs of houses, while men and older boys escorted us the length of the street. On the far side of the barricade a young man in a bright blue shirt kept pace with us as we went. Others in Arab dress stared across at us. In some places the wire was down to the level of the ground. Easy enough to step across! Yet to have done so would have been to invite death. It was a moslem village, but both the school and the Mosque were on the Israel side. They hoped to build new ones soon, they told us. So the men talked. And now some of the women and children had joined us, following behind in silence. As we were leaving amid salaams and bows and kissing of hands, an Arab on the Israel side of the wire waved to us, then said something. 'I thought they mustn't communicate,' I said to the policeman. He smiled. 'They're not supposed to. Sometimes a blind eye is turned.'

'But what did he say?' I asked.

'He said, "See what Allah has done to us!" ' the policeman answered.

'Has anyone ever come across . . . escaped, I mean?' one of the Americans asked. The policeman repeated the question to the 'patriarch' in the blue *abaya*, then interpreted his answer. 'One man did,' was the reply. 'We could not hide him, so we sent him back. It was the only thing we could do.'

'Have the Arabs here ill-feeling against those in Israel,' the Frenchman asked.

Again the question was put to the old man and his answer interpreted: 'What is the sense of ill-feeling? We must accept the will of Allah.'

The Arab who is a Moslem speaks of the 'Will of Allah', the Christian Arab of the 'Will of God'. 'It is God's Will for us,' said a refugee working at the Franciscans' printing press in Jerusalem. 'God wills it,' said an elderly resident in the American Colony, 'Our Lord suffered, so we must.' He had owned much property, had been a man of great possessions: now he was living on fast depleting capital.

The Arab, if his spirit has not been broken, bears his afflictions with dignity and patience to which a western Christian may not attain in a lifetime. At its best the resignation of the Arab is saintly. At its worst it is a stultifying fatalism that becomes an excuse for doing nothing to fight evil or alleviate suffering.

CHAPTER XXIV

Mount Nebo and Jerash

I

EAST of the Jordan there was a sense of wind-swept space and of time going back to before the world began. . . . Mountains reached away, fold upon fold of them, cut by dried water-courses – the Arabs call them *wadis* – with steep, rock-strewn sides. And there was the desert: not flat unending sand, but burnt-out sandy soil covered in places with a black shell of lava that glittered in the sun like jet. When a wind blew the sand rose in drifting columns. At times there would appear the great walls and rounded arches of some forgotten Umayyad palace. The expanse of sky seemed larger than elsewhere, and the stars to shine with an especial brilliance.

Even in the burning August noon a wind blew on the flinty ridge of Nebo. I stood there, where they tell you Moses stood as he looked across at the Promised Land. Away to the west I saw the green line of the Jordan meet the turquoise and frosted white of the Dead Sea, with, beyond, the oasis that is Jericho, and the mountains of Judah. To the north the mountains of Ephraim merged into those of Gilead, and Hermon was a sapphire blur.

A few yards away was a ruined Byzantine church. The sunlight glittered on the apse and broken pillars. A Bedouin with a small brush in his hand appeared as if from nowhere and began to sweep away the sand that protected the mosaic floor. A little replica of the church revealed itself, then a basket of bread, then a gazelle wearing a collar and bell, then the hindquarters of a lion. . . . Close to the church were the remains of monastic buildings: a courtyard and cells for hermits, and a cistern with ovens. Among the tumble-down walls a mare was tethered. She came up whinnying. The Arab reached out his hand and taking hold of the halter drew her close to me.

Nebo seemed to belong to the Bedouins. I saw, at least, no other human creatures. It was a Bedouin woman – again appearing as though from nowhere – who led me up the mountain slope to see the mosaics that once were the floor of a church dedicated to the Saints Lot and Procopius. Arab women have often a closed-in, secretive expression. This woman's face, however, was shining as if with a happiness that could not contain itself. Structurally, too, it was a beautiful face: the cheek-bones were high, but not too high; the eyes deep-set, the brow low and broad. The lips, even in repose, seemed to smile. When she greeted me, she bent low over my hand – her silver bangles jingling – kissed it, then touched it with her brow. There were tattoo marks on her face and a gold ring in her nostril. Thick, dark plaits hung forward over each shoulder. Bands of magenta embroidery decorated her black dress; the sleeves, too, were magenta. Her elder child wore a dress like her mother's, but with green embroidery and green sleeves. The younger was in a terra-cotta garment, more a tunic than a dress. Both had their mother's features, but whereas the elder was grave and thoughtful, the younger laughed and chattered, putting out her hands (the nails were stained with henna) to finger my dress and touch my watch.

A wooden shed protected the mosaic floor. To see it to better advantage the woman swilled water on to it, then wiped it with a cloth. The effect was that of light flung upon a dark picture or patterned carpet. What had been dim a moment before was shining and clear in detail. Eagerly, the children pointed now to this, now to that. Men bringing in the harvest. A shepherd with his flock. A fisherman. A bear. A tiger. Rabbits. Ducks and geese and long-legged wading birds. And in front of where the altar must have stood, two lambs on either side of the Tree of Life.

I walked down the mountainside with the woman and her children. The hot wind bent the squills and withered grasses. Black goats were grazing, and a shepherd boy played on a pipe of reeds.

II

Each ruined city has its own character. Ashkelon goes back to a black, mysterious past. Caesarea, in two broken statues, recalls the solemn splendour of Rome.

Jerash is more civilized than Ashkelon, more elegant than Caesarea. Her past is a long one: some say the city was founded by Alexander the Great; others by Perdiccas, one of his generals; others attribute its beginnings to Ptolemy II who changed Amman into the Hellenistic Philadelphia. After Pompey's settlement of the east, Jerash became one of the cities of the league called the Decapolis. From then it increased in power, wealth and luxury. Time passed. Pagan temples gave place to Byzantine churches built, some of them, from the stones of the temples and of a splendour so excessive as to seem to invite destruction. And destruction came. First the Persians, then the Arabs, then earthquakes. . . . And yet, as I looked at what was left of the city lying broken there among the red mountains of Gilead, with no habitation near but a mud-built Circassian village, it seemed to me that the past of Jerash lay lightly upon her – that her mood was one almost of gaiety.

The mountains were parched, but among the ruins trees were growing, lending to the scene a gracious beauty. A breeze silvered the poplar leaves and sunlight glinted on the dark shiny foliage of fig trees heavy with fruit. Oleander blossoms showed scarlet through vistas of pillars. On the banks of a stream – the Greeks used to call it the Golden River – walnut trees grew in profusion. Linnets twittered among them, or a jay would flash its claret breast and blue-barred wings.

I walked along the Street of the Columns that runs the city's length, from south to north. The huge paving stones were cut by the wheels of chariots, squills grew up from between them. The Arab major walked at my side, his blue forage-cap sitting jauntily on hair stiff as a badger's coat, his fingers moving over the amber beads of his Moslem 'rosary'. There are thirty-three beads, each representing three names of Allah. Ninety-nine names in all. The hundredth name is a secret known only to the camel – hence the camel's air of superiority.

On either side, the street was lined with pillars. Ionic, then Corinthian. They reached on and on, seeming to disappear into a fold of the hills. They gave a feeling of space and order, leisure and time without end.

Wherever I looked there were ruins. A triumphal arch. A temple of Zeus. Pillars of Artemis' shrine, lonely without the roof that once they supported. Baths. Porticos. A theatre. A nymphaeum with elaborate conch decorations. Side by side with these, and, except for the expert, hardly distinguishable from them were shattered churches dedicated to Saint George and Saint Procopius, Saints Cosmas and Damian, Saint Peter and Saint Paul. In front of the church of Saint Theodore a fountain court was strewn with marbles: here, year after year, used to be re-enacted the miracle of the changing of the water into wine. A flight of steps led up through a gateway, then between columns, to the cathedral shrine dedicated to the mother of Christ and the Archangels Michael and Gabriel: as I went up two Arab children darted from behind the pillars, shouting to one another in shrill voices that echoed back mysteriously.

Everywhere the ground was littered with fragments of marble: petal-white, violet, golden-brown and a mottled red that glittered with diamonds: even the dust was powdered marble.

A great oval of Ionic pillars enclosed the flagged forum, with, in its centre, a plinth for a statue. I looked from a distance at these pillars, some of them broken and standing alone, the rest linked one to another by a slender architrave. Then I went down and walked among them, laying my hand on their polished surface, looking up at their capitals brown as sugar against the sky.

The sun dropped, deepening the red of the mountains and touching the pillars with gold. Day gave way to twilight. A white moon hung in a violet sky. The sky darkened, and the white moon turned to silver.

Arches and columns, larger and paler than by day, flung black, clear-cut shadows. Leaves scraped in the breeze and cicadas kept up a rhythm that was hard and unbroken.

III

The road from Jerash to Amman went over the mountains, then across the Zerka that in the Bible they call the Jabbok. At every bend the Arab major leant forward, restraining his young driver (a corporal in the Legion) with a 'shushing' sound, as though he were chiding an obstreperous child.

We passed through a forest of little larch trees, delicately pale in the light of the moon, then stopped in a clearing where Bedouins were encamped. As we got out of the car, dogs came up barking. A lean-faced man called them off, and made us welcome. He was wearing a deep brown *abayah*, and he had a silver-handled dagger at his waist. An old wrinkled woman crouched in the darkness of the tent, smoking a pipe with a long straight stem. A young woman came forward and kissed my hand. To the Bedouins, as to the Homeric Greeks, strangers and wayfarers are under the protection of God. They have a saying: 'Are we not all the guests of Allah?' Not to share Allah's gifts would be to sin against heaven.

I sat there in the shadows understanding nothing that was said around me, yet at home, sipping coffee that had a faint taste of smoke and eating a great circle of bread, thin as a wafer, freshly baked over the fire on a piece of sheet-iron that looked like the lid of a dust-bin. Outside, the moon touched the larch trees with silver.

The Bedouins, or Badawins, are a nomadic people: the word means dwellers in el Badia, the desert. They pitch their long brown tents wherever they hope to find vegetation and water for their sheep and goats, horses and camels.

Their sheep are the fat-tailed Palestinian breed, so named because they store up fat in their tails to last through the lean dry summer. The goats are dark brown, almost black, with silky coats; drooping ears, and horns that bend back or sideways, twisting, sometimes, like a corkscrew.

The Bedouins' horses are graceful creatures of a slender build with long manes and tails. To possess a horse is a matter of dignity and self-respect. The animal is greatly treasured: a yearling mare can be valued at the worth of ten camels. Foals are fed on camel's milk as well as on that of the mother, and for the full-grown animals camels are used to bring fodder and water from neighbouring villages. Horses are carefully watched and tended, for they easily become lame when travelling over the burning gravelly soil of the desert – there is also the risk of their being stolen. White is the favourite colour, but those of a yellowish strain are said to be the fastest. Except for carrying out a short, sharp raid, the horse is of little practical value. He is, however, the answer to a poetical need that is deep in the nature of the Bedouin.

The camel, on the other hand, is essential to a life that is lived in the desert. Camel's milk is a valuable food, whether taken fresh or made into *leben.* Its flesh, too, can be eaten, that of the young animal, especially if it comes from the hump, being looked upon as a delicacy. The hair, which is collected in the spring, is made into material, pillows and ropes. Mixed with sheep's wool and the hair of goats, it is woven into the rough worsted that is used for the Bedouin tent or 'house of hair'. The hide makes bottles, bags and harness. Sometimes, too, if money is needed to buy weapons or clothing, a camel is sold to a trader or peasant who uses the animal for carrying burdens or ploughing. Among the Bedouins a man's wealth is counted in the number of his camels: a rich sheikh may own a thousand, a poor herdsman not more than one or two.

The camel can cover great distances without ill-effects. Its long legs move at a fine pace, and the big feet with their spongy, cushion-like pads are adapted to ground that would split the hooves of a horse or ox. Further, it stores fat in its hump and is able to drink quantities of water, when opportunity arises, then go without for a considerable stretch of time. A large camel can sometimes be induced to drink sixty quarts before setting out on a journey, nor does it object to bitter-tasting water that a horse would not touch. Its food is what it can find in the desert – scrub, the salt-tasting tamarisk, and the prickly caper plant.

The hump is an indication of the camel's state of health. If the animal is unwell or undernourished, the hump shrinks. With a return to health, it resumes its normal size.

The camel is said to sleep little. It is true that it closes its eyes and lays its long neck on the ground, but soon it is sitting up again, chewing its cud. It pastures by night as well as day, looking in the light of the moon like a great white ghost. It needs to be watched while feeding, for it is inclined to wander away: for this reason one of its fore-legs, sometimes, is bent up and fastened by a rope.

The camel's saddle is an enormous contraption consisting of two arches made of mimosa wood, each surmounted by a knob. These are joined by cross-pieces that are spread with sheep-skins and padded cushions. The rider guides the beast by a single rein attached to a halter: sometimes he taps it on the neck with a stick. Whether through stupidity or, more likely, an inborn aloofness, the camel rarely answers to a name or shows recognition of its owner.

Mahommed said that God created no better animal, and that at the third blast of the trumpet on the Day of Judgement, the faithful would be borne to heaven on winged, milk-white camels with saddles of gold.

CHAPTER XXV

Petra

I

THE plump man with the rings on his fingers sighed and took out a cigar.

'I'm here three days . . . not a girl, not a cabaret.' He was a film producer, and with him was his manager who might have passed for Clarke Gable. We were on the balcony of the Amman Club Hotel overlooking the street. There was a fracas going on below, a demonstration concerning the Arabs in Morocco. A couple of shops had been burnt out and stones thrown. Arab Legionaries with fixed bayonets stood on the pavement, and police were hurrying off a struggling youth.

Amman was noisy, restless and hot. Traffic blocked the streets. The pavements were crowded. Desert Arabs strode by. Swaggering Legionaries flashed black eyes from under red and white or primrose *keffiyehs* as they elbowed their way among men wearing tarbushes, European suits and a wealth of rings. There were veiled Moslem women; Bedouin women with thick silky plaits and tribal marks tattooed on cheeks and chin; and women, too, who wore nylons and dresses *à la Parisienne*.

Flat-roofed, characterless houses straggled up and down hills divided by steep valleys, and dust rose in clouds from buildings not yet completed. The royal palace had a wall and trees about it. There was a mosque, a Franciscan church, a cinema which advertised itself with crudely-coloured posters, and on the outskirts of the town villas and legations and a second, newly built palace. It seemed at first sight a place without a past. But this impression was false. Amman was formerly called Rabath or Rabath Ammon, and was first mentioned in Deuteronomy as possessing the bed of Og, King of Bashan: 'For only Og, King of Bashan remained of the race of giants. His bed of iron is shown, which is in Rabath of the children of Ammon, being nine cubits long, and four broad after the measure of a man's hand'.

Moreover, it was while fighting at Amman that Uriah the Hittite met his death through the scheming of King David.

In later years the town received the name Philadelphia, and in 63 B.C., became one of the cities of the Decapolis. The ruins of Jupiter's temple are on the acropolis, and opposite the Philadelphia Hotel, in earshot of the traffic, a splendid Roman theatre lies at the foot of a hill topped with the modern houses. I was disappointed when I saw the theatre for the first time. It was behind a barrier of wire, and near-by buildings dwarfed its size. I thought it looked dreary. Then I saw it from above, at night. It was spread there under the hill in the full light of the moon, the seats rising tier upon tier with gangways intersecting: it looked like a great milk-white shell.

* * *

I had come to Amman in the hope of visiting Petra.

My mind was haunted with memories of what I had read of this mysterious rock city – at once Roman, Greek and Nabataean – lying in the shadow of Mount Hor, where Aaron, they say, was buried – and with 'high places' of its own going back to the Canaanite worship of Baal. It is Selah (the word means 'the cliff') of the Old Testament, the capital of Edom. The Greek name Petra is recent by comparison, and seldom used by the Arabs who speak of the district as the Valley of Moses. For over a thousand years Petra was lost to the world, its site unknown to the people of the west. Then, in 1812 John Burckhardt, a Swiss, found his way there. To allay the suspicions of the Arabs, he pretended that he was a Moslem who wanted to sacrifice a goat in sight of Mount Hor. Even so, he had to cut short his time. Dean Stanley went to Petra in 1853. Edward Lear intended to spend a week there, but was attacked by Arabs and had to make a hurried departure after one night. Lear was entranced by what he saw. Doughty, on the other hand, describes it in *Arabia Deserta* as 'a wild abysmal place . . . strange and horrible as a pit'.

I talked about going to Petra to the Arab major who had shown me Jerash. He was prepared to help me. However, a military mission arrived from Egypt, and I saw no more of him. Then I asked an English brigadier with whom I was having dinner. 'There's no means of getting there,' he said, 'and nothing to make the journey worth while. Only blazing sun and rock. Better abandon the idea.' It was plain that he looked on me as an eccentric who was aping Gertrude Bell or Lady Hester Stanhope!

I made enquiries in the hotel, then in a travel agency, as well as in a number of shops. The answer was always the same. Nobody visits Petra in August, I was told: the heat would be unbearable. The time to go was between September and April, when there were trips arranged from Amman and the greater part of the journey covered by air.

With Petra still in my mind, I was looking through the wire barricade at the Roman theatre, when a voice at my side said: 'I show you the theatre?'

'No,' I answered crossly.

'I show you the country . . . Jerash . . . the sights? I drive a car.'

'I've been to Jerash and I don't want to see the sights,' I said yet more crossly. Then I looked at the speaker. He had a round, good-tempered face, curly hair, and honest, rather protruding eyes. He was smoking a pipe.

'What about Petra?' I asked him suddenly.

'Petra?' he echoed. 'Petra is a long way . . . the wrong time of the year and very hot.'

We talked on. The end of it was that José – he was, he told me, an Arab refugee and had formerly owned a garage in Haifa – was willing to drive me to Petra at a reduced charge if I would agree to travel both ways by night. This would prevent his losing two days custom in Amman. He had done the same thing, he assured me, for some girls at the American Embassy; he had also driven for the British Consulate.

'I am respectable, to be trusted,' he added in a faintly offended tone, seeing, I imagine, my hesitation to come to a decision. 'I can arrange all,' he went on. 'The car . . . the food . . . a horse for the last part of the journey.'

'I'll let you know if you call this afternoon,' I told him.

I thought the matter over. It would have been easier if I could have found a companion. There was no one in the hotel I could ask to go with me, unless the plump man with the rings: I did not imagine that he would be an asset.

I talked to a woman I knew in a bookshop. 'I don't like the idea,' she said. 'You know nothing of the driver.' She was only echoing my own uneasiness. He might murder me, fling me into a ravine. A hundred hair-raising suppositions came to my mind. And yet I had set my heart on going. How cowardly and unadventurous I would seem when I returned to England, regretting that I had flung away this one chance of seeing Petra. Besides, José looked trustworthy. The round, good-natured face and the pipe inspired me with confidence. I was thinking on these lines when a woman in the bookshop broke in. 'Why not ring the British Consulate and ask if they know your driver?'

I followed her advice, not without misgivings. The Consulate might well take the view of the brigadier, that the idea was crazy. However, the male voice that answered was sympathetic. It would be a thousand pities, I was told, to go back to England without having seen Petra. As to the driver – well, one could not, of course, be sure. But car drivers in Amman were a carefully chosen lot. It would not be to his advantage to murder his fare! 'Tell him!' he went on, 'that you rang the Consulate'.

II

The open country rolled away to the far distance. Arabs were driving home their asses and sheep and goats. To the west a flame-red sunset gave place to a blaze of gold. Then the whole sky became a misty purple in which a few stars glinted. In the east the moon hung like a crystal ball lit from within. Fires twinkled in Bedouin encampments and lights shone from farmsteads enclosed within fortress-like walls.

We stopped at Madaba, where the Latin church crowns the ancient acropolis. On the mosaic floor of the Greek church there is the oldest existing map of Palestine. It shows Damascus and Byblos in the north, Alexandria in the south and to the east Amman and Petra. At Jericho there are palm trees laden with dates. A ship sails on the Jordan and golden fish swim in its waters. Hills appear dark, valleys light. A *wadi* cuts down a mountainside to the Dead Sea. Jerusalem is depicted with its walls, battlements and towers. What is now called the Damascus Gate has a large pillar inside it, which explains its Arabic name, Bab-el-Amud: the Gate of the Column.

Somewhere beyond Madaba, Roman columns jutted against the sky. There was a wonderful feeling of space, and an infinite silence. . . . Now and again I was beset with misgivings at having set out on this strange adventure. Then I looked at the stolid figure of José, and dismissed my fears.

Kerak is the impregnable fortress that is called Kir Harash in the Old Testament. It is also the town of the savage Renault de Chatillon who used to make onslaughts on the Moslem pilgrims on their way to Mecca. The castle hung there upon the mountainside, in the light of the moon. It was like an enchanted castle. I almost hoped that I would never see it again: it could not have the same dreamlike quality a second time. Below, the lights of the town glittered.

We stopped at the police post to show my passport, and were entertained with cups of hot mint tea. A little later we stopped again on a level stretch of road, to have supper.

José spread a cloth on the seat in the back of the car, and laid my meal before me: tinned ham, hard-boiled eggs, cucumbers, bananas, tomatoes, olives, grapes, flat circles of bread and a bottle of water.

The road went on and on, with on either side a landscape that reached away mysteriously, and overhead, the white ball of the moon. I became sleepy, yet fought against sleep for fear of missing anything. Even so, I slept soundly but intermittently. Each time I woke we were crossing one of the *wadis* over which the road runs between Amman and Petra.

So strange a sight met my eyes, that it was hard to tell whether what I saw was real or the shreds of a dream from which I had not yet fully awakened. The moon was more brilliant than ever. It shone down on mountains that leapt skywards, then dropped into unfathomable valleys. The mountains had a ghastly pallor, like faces under neon lighting. They were creased and gashed with shadows; every ravine and gully was visible. There seemed no end to the mountains. They reached away, one beyond the other. And below, in the valleys, what by day would have been the course of a river, or an oasis of green, looked now like an ink-black serpent twisting its way among the corpse-white rocks. The sky, pricked with faint stars and drenched in the light of the moon, was gentle above the savagery of the mountains.

The road climbed up and up, then dropped again with disconcerting suddenness. It was white and narrow. Stones strewed the way, and boulders hung above as though about to fall. On one side towering rock, on the other a drop to the valley below. At one moment we seemed to head for a precipice, at another it was as if a wall of rock barred our way. There was no vegetation except squills, pale and ghostly as the cliffs on which, as if by a miracle, they had taken root. Sometimes the moon hid its face behind the mountains, and then stared at us anew. I closed my eyes in terror, then opened them, rebuking myself for missing anything of this macabre scene. It was like a Blake picture.

The lights of a car flashed from across the valley, vanished and then were upon us, suddenly, round a bend, dazzlingly bright. It was a road made long years ago for caravans and camels. There was scarcely room to pass. Again, I closed my eyes. When I opened them, the car had gone and I saw a camel ridden by a figure swathed in white. The animal looked pale and huge. I could see the tassels on its head. Its eyes glinted green, and its underlip protruded arrogantly.

I slept again, then woke in a place of steep deserted streets, barred windows and houses that flung square black shadows. There were olive trees on a slope: their leaves in the moonlight looked like pewter. I heard running water, or imagined I heard it. We stopped. A figure wearing a *keffiyeh* and carrying a staff spoke to José through the window; his eyes were dark and his teeth flashed white. He was the town watchman and we were in Tafileh.

We moved on in the blue, milky light of the moon. Somewhere away to the right was Bosra in the land of the Edomites. My thoughts, moving in a world between sleeping and waking, turned now to Lawrence of Arabia, now to the prophet Isaiah.

'Who is it that cometh from Edom, with dyed garments from Bosra, this beautiful one in his robe, walking in the greatness of his strength?'

Still we went on. We stopped – I do not know how long afterwards – outside a flat-looking building with closed shutters and a wall about it. It stood there under the moon grim and lonely: it was another police post at which security regulations required us to report. José got out and rapped on the door. There was no answer. He knocked again. No sound but the muffled stamp of a horse in a stable. 'I'll sleep for an hour,' he said. 'If no one answers then, we'll go on.' He put up the windows of the car. 'In case of Bedouins,' he said, and settled himself in the front with a rifle at his side. Soon he was snoring. The heat was stifling. I opened the door and slipped out into the cool, sweet air. Again there was the sense of infinite space – the countryside reaching away in the opal moonlight.

The distant baying of a dog broke upon the stillness, and I could see the long black shapes of Bedouin tents and the glint of a fire. On the far horizon the dawn showed silver-pale. I took a rug out of the car and spreading it on the sandy ground sat with my back against the wall of the police post. Amman was far behind and Petra was yet to come. At the end of an hour José knocked as before. Again, the stamp of a horse. 'We'll get on,' he said. Again I slept.

* * *

It was day when I woke. The sun was shining, and the sky a clear bright blue. The moon was still there, but it had a shrunken look, like a withered magnolia. Near at hand the landscape was reddish-brown and flat. Then it rolled away in undulating stony hills that overlapped one another or dipped into purple-shadowed hollows. In the far distance there were mountains pencilled against the sky. They were claret-coloured but splashed with deep violet and sapphire: after the pallor of the moonlight the colours were breath-taking. On either side of the road camels were feeding – more camels than I had ever seen or imagined to see. I counted over fifty, then gave up. Some were large, some small; some handsome, some scraggy. A few were as white as milk. Most of them were the colour of sand. Others had a mottled, patchy appearance. A little Bedouin girl was keeping watch. A couple of the animals straggled on to the road: the car slowed down to pass.

We came to a stretch of country covered with a thick low-growing scrub. A covey of partridges dashed across our path with a flurry of wings. In a moment José was out of the car, crouching, his rifle to his shoulder. He fired. I was glad that he failed to get a bird.

We dropped downhill through a gorge with great lime-stone rocks that reminded me of Burrington Combe, then stopped for breakfast near the Well of Musa. Saint Jerome was referring, perhaps, to this when he wrote that in his day a cliff was shown near Petra which, when struck, 'yielded water in plenty'. It is a lovely well, enclosed in a rock chamber, with deep cool springs and water gushing over stones. We drank the water, filled our bottles, and washed our faces, then sat down a little distance away under the shadow of a boulder. We ate more hard-boiled eggs, with bread, apples, and bananas, and slices of melon that we first cooled by standing it in the spring water.

As we sat there Bedouins brought their animals to drink. There were sheep and goats, small dark-faced cows and numbers of asses. Some of the asses were mushroom-coloured, some grey, some chocolate-brown with pale rings round their eyes. An olive-skinned boy was holding the bridle of an elegant, dappled grey horse. A girl, bare-footed and wearing a black dress embroidered with green, was having trouble with an enormous camel which was taking itself off in the opposite direction to the rest. No amount of shouting or beating or thumping had effect. It changed its course only when surrounded by half a dozen screaming, scolding children, and then leisurely and with a look of patronizing disdain.

We continued downhill to Al Ji, to the police post which was the usual flat building enclosed by a wall. It stood on a plateau above the level of the village. We were greeted in the courtyard by two men in khaki uniform wearing primrose *keffiyehs* and black highly polished riding boots: they took us into what seemed to be an office where we drank glasses of hot sweet tea. We sat on. Time seemed to be of no account.

* * *

It must have been about eight o'clock when the four of us went out into the blazing sunshine. Below us, in the distance were the mountains that I had seen earlier that morning. I knew that beyond them was Petra.

We walked down a dusty slope to where two boys were waiting with a horse. It was a flea-bitten grey, with a long mane and tail: an old animal, but Arab horses keep their grace even in age. It had a high saddle, an embroidered black and red saddle-cloth, and a bridle decorated with white shells. One of the police made a sign to me to get up. I had no riding clothes: the full skirt of my pink and white dress fell in folds on either side of the horse's flanks. And so, accompanied by the boys on foot, I set out on the last lap of the journey to Petra.

The elder boy, who was my guide, wore khaki jodhpurs and a red and white *keffiyeh*. He had a cartridge belt round his waist, and a rifle slung over his shoulder. We had not gone far before he took off the rifle and began swinging it over his head as though he were performing some kind of ritual dance. His lean, brown face was shrewd and full of mischief. He spoke English fairly well. The younger boy, who was carrying bottles of water and a knapsack full of fruit and bread, kept up a conversation in Arabic, addressing himself now to his companion, now to me.

We went through the twisting street of Al Ji. There was a certain amount of stone-work, but most of the houses were of mud. Figs and olives grew on terraced slopes, and there were cattle in an enclosure of rough stones.

Men squatting in doorways stared as we went by, and women passed with bundles on their heads. A boy riding a donkey thrust so close to me that a water-tin on the animal's back jabbed my shin, grazing the skin. The boy burst out laughing, whereupon my guide turned on him, brandishing the rifle and letting out a spate of words. We continued downhill, and out on to an open plain.

Here so weird a sight met my eyes that I wanted, for a moment, to go not a yard further. At the outer edges of the plain there were sinister formations of sandstone – pale and bleached, as though all colour had been drained from them. Some were square and flat-topped; others rounded; like lumps of dough that had been fossilized. Some, again, were hollowed into natural caves or cut into tombs that looked like eye-sockets in a skull. Others were carved into towers decorated with a vertical or horizontal groove. In front of me stood massive obelisks. The heat came down, mercilessly, from the hard blue sky, and up from the dazzling chalk-white ground: it was flung back, wave upon wave of it, from the blinding death-pale rocks.... We went on and on, the sun beating on us. The horse clinked its bit. The boys were silent.

Suddenly, a mountain-wall blocked our path: violet-coloured, but streaked with blue and crimson and green, and dappled with shadows. The colour was restful to the eyes after the white glaring plain. And, again, suddenly, as if by magic, a way opened: we were in the ravine which is called Siq.

It was cool, almost cold. Cliffs rose on either side, vast and terrible, sometimes meeting so close overhead as almost to hide the sky. They were red sandstone, a red that changed with every flicker of light, every shadow. Sometimes it was a pale clear red, then again, a deep rose that darkened to purple or blazed into orange. Trees and shrubs grew out from the rocks, junipers, oleanders and figs, broom and the trailing blue-leaved caper plant. The Siq is a dried-up river bed, its floor deep in pebbles. It was also the highway into Petra; at one time the emporium of the Levant. Through it the caravans from the east used to come, laden with silks and ivories and spices, on their way to Gaza and Alexandria and the world of Greece and Rome.

Its intense silence was accentuated by every sound: the scrunch of the horse's hooves, the jingle of the bit, the clap of a pigeon's wings. Suddenly, too, there was a sweet shrill cry from a flight of small black-plumaged birds that now clustered on a boulder, now rose, now settled again. The elder boy put his rifle to his shoulder. The younger one hurriedly signalled me to dismount. I did as I was told. A shot rang out, echoing down the rocky corridor. The horse threw up its head and scuffled its hooves on the pebbles. The birds scattered, screaming but unhurt. This procedure was repeated three and four times. But after the first time, I refused to budge from the horse – at which the younger boy pulled a wry face and flung out his hands despairingly.

We went on, the pebbles scrunching, the gorge now widening, now narrowing, and overhead a strip of sky startlingly blue above the red towering rocks. In one place a six-branched candlestick was carved on the face of the cliff. There were niches as though for statues, and what looked like little shrines with a classical pillar on either side and a pediment above; or flights of steps would suddenly appear, going nowhere, coming from nowhere. The atmosphere was strange: it was secretive and empty – utterly empty, except for the boys and myself, the horse, and the birds. Yet it seemed to be possessed by invisible beings, by unseen watching eyes, so that I was thankful for the boys and for the flea-bitten grey, clinking her bit and snuffing the air.

The Siq ended in a burst of light. There in front of me, cut into the rose-red cliff and seeming to rise out of a tangle of oleanders, was the tomb that has come to be called the *Khazneh*, or the treasury of Pharoah. Four classical pillars, two on either side, supported an architrave with over it a pediment, and above this, so as to form a second story, more pillars and in the centre a lantern upholding an urn.

The colour of the stone was dazzlingly bright, but most striking of all was the contrast between the sophistication of the carving and the rough rock that enclosed it like an immense frame.

From the *Khazneh* a bridle path went northward to a great open space. Ahead I saw mountain-like rocks rising from a plain of purply-red earth. To the west there was a huge Roman theatre, to the east a cliff cut into tombs with carved fronts.

Petra is a place of wonder. Elsewhere there are ruins of temples, palaces and tombs. The difference is that here they are cut into the natural rock, have no existence apart from it: so that, in a real sense, Petra is a rock city, not a city built of stone quarried from rock. Most of the buildings are in the classical style. But there are others that go back to an earlier Assyrian tradition: often the sole decoration is a horizontal line of crow-step carving.

Another wonder is the colour of the sandstone which ranges from a dark earth-red to rose, rose to a lurid flame, flame to the red of blood. Engrained in it are surprising shades of violet, china blue, yellow, ivory, indigo, raspberry and coral. Sometimes these merge into one another, like paints on a palate; or they remain distinct, forming clear-cut rings or twirling sugarstick patterns, each adding a fresh brightness. No wonder that Edward Lear's servant, Georgio, exclaimed to his master that here was 'a world made of chocolate, ham, curry powder and salmon!'

Another wonder of Petra is its utter desolation: as though the city had been visited by an overwhelming disaster: had been, all in one moment, abandoned by its inhabitants, abandoned by its gods.

The younger boy stayed with the horse, while with the elder I clambered up rocks, pushing my way through tamarisks and fig trees and oleanders, stopping from time to time to take breath or to marvel at the precipice still reaching above me. My companion went ahead, moving at a fine pace, nimble as a goat. I would lose sight of him, then, in the silence, hear his voice calling back to me: it had a shrill wild note, like the cry of a bird, ringing out from the cliffs. Each time I lost sight of him, I was afraid. Then he would come back, leaping down, careless yet sure-footed, holding out to me a thin brown hand. He carried my bag for me, and, snatching off my straw hat he replaced it by his own *keffiyeh*, fastening it with the camel-hair strings: the rest of the trip he wore my hat and was mighty pleased with it.

Steep paths and great uneven steps that lose themselves in a tangle of growth lead up to the 'high places' of Petra, where once the worshippers of Baal soaked the earth with the blood of their victims. The altar of slaying is there and the altar of burnt offering. Pools, for ritual ablutions, are cut in the rock.

* * *

In the heat of the afternoon I sat near the Roman theatre on a boulder with overhead a fig tree reaching out its shade. The boys were with me and the horse tethered near by. I could see the broken seats of the theatre rising tier on tier and in the cliff above them gaping tombs. This was the scene that Edward Lear had been painting when hostile Arabs swooped on him from the heights. I felt weighed down by the past: a dark, silent past reaching back, beyond the Romans, to the Nabataeans – those strange people who, coming from the southern deserts of Arabia, had possessed themselves of this rock stronghold, turning it into a city of temples and tombs where nature and sophistication met.

The harsh high-pitched voice of my guide broke in upon my thoughts. He asked question after question. Where did I live? Had I parents? A brother? A husband? Did I like Petra? Did I like Jordan as well as London? All I said was interpreted to the younger one who lay on his stomach, his face resting on his hands, his eyes staring at me.

The boys and the horse were the only link with the world of familiar things. And they, too, seemed unreal. The horse, with its shabby elegant trappings, might have come out of a dream; and the boys were wild creatures whom I could not visualize in other surroundings.

We had sat, perhaps, half an hour when the elder leapt to his feet. 'I fetch water,' he said. Before I realized what had happened the pair of them were astride the horse and out of sight. I heard their voices coming from a distance, faint and unreal. I was alone with the empty theatre and the tombs. My guide was gone, the horse was gone. So, too, I remembered, was my bag which the boy was still carrying, and in it my passport and money.

After a moment of anger with myself for having let this happen, and, then, for distrusting the boys, the matter of the passport and money troubled me surprisingly little. It was as nothing to the terror of the silence: a nightmare terror of blood-red rocks under a glaring sky. Again, the past was with me: a savage, barbaric past. Between Then and Now there was no link.

I looked at my watch. The boys had been away perhaps ten minutes, but it seemed an hour. I called out, hoping that I might hear that strange, bird-like voice in answer. But it was my own voice that came back, flung at me from the rocks.

I clambered down from where I was sitting, then up a slope to a tomb with a front carved from rainbow-streaked stone. Its pillars had an almost liquid quality, as though they were melting into the rock from which they were hewn: they made me think of gutted candles. I laid my hand on one of them: the sandstone crumbled under my touch. Then, I went into the darkness, feeling almost an intruder as I did so. A bird flew out, nearly brushing my face. The roof of natural rock was black with streaks of white and coral pink; there was a smell of goats and the air was dank. I came out into the sun beating down on the rocks. Overhead a golden-brown eagle soared. It was then I heard a voice. I strained my ears to listen. It came again. Then I saw the flea-bitten grey and the boys on her back: the terror was gone: the terror of the silence, and of a past that was always present. And yet not wholly gone – rather, kept at bay by companionship both human and animal.

* * *

That evening we stopped again at the spring of Musa, when the animals were gathering to drink. A huge cream-coloured camel kneeling by the water was turning its neck from side to side, like a swan. It had red and silver tassels on its head. Its owner was resplendent in an *abayah* that was a deep night-blue embroidered with silver. His lean handsome face brought to my mind the picture of Auda Abu Tay in *The Seven Pillars of Wisdom.* I noticed with what ease he mounted his camel, stepping on it from behind and losing nothing of his grace or balance when the animal heaved itself into standing position. He rode away, followed by his wife in black, riding a smaller beast, then two sons on asses. Earlier I had watched the boys quarrelling while they fetched water from the spring. In a flash one had whipped out a silver-handled knife, with a fierce curved blade. There were sharp words until the father with more sharp words, yet unruffled dignity, commanded them to separate.

After the imprisoning rocks of Petra, I was glad of the open rolling country. We stopped by a stream, ate goat's cheese and bread, and put what was left of the melon into the water to be cool for later on the journey. In the distance I could see the mountains that I had looked at in the morning. They were a deep, mysterious blue, and above them the first stars glimmered. In the distance a gazelle passed with graceful bounding shape. I gave myself up to the immense quiet of the evening – content, in that the impossible had happened, and I had seen Petra.

* * *

Massive stone walls stood upon the treeless hillside casting their shadows under the moon. It was Shobeck, stronghold of the Crusaders. There was a wedding in the town. While we drank coffee at the police post, we could hear music and merry-making and rifle shots. Then, as we drove away, we were held up by the procession. It straggled across the street; crowds shouting and singing and beating drums. Figures in white held lamps high over their heads and torches flared.

Then on and up the mountain road, with below, the moon-silvered valleys.

We stopped again at the foot of a *wadi*, at a coffee-house among a wilderness of figs and poplar trees. We sat under a shelter with a bamboo roof where we were brought glasses of tea by a man wearing pyjamas. He showed no surprise at our arrival between three and four in the morning. He was glad, he said, of company: few travellers passed that way. The air was moist and stifling. Bats flittered and mosquitoes whined.

Suddenly I heard a low, wailing note. On a rock a few yards away from me I saw the small plump shape of an owl, its body bowing in time to its music. It was the Little Owl common in the English countryside: the *Athene Noctua*, sacred to Athens and to Pallas Athene, goddess of Athens. The Arabs call the bird the *boomeh*. It was introduced to England from the Levant in the last century, by Lord Lilford.

* * *

The sky was pale with the dawn as we drove through the empty streets of Amman. With José at my side I climbed the steep steps to the hotel. He rang the bell, then shook me by the hand. . . . Ibraham opened the door. By day he was at the reception desk, with a smiling face. At five in the morning he was smiling and unperturbed. 'Madame, was Petra good?' he said.

I followed him into the kitchen where I drank glass after glass of cold water. I had not booked a room (for I was going to Jerusalem that morning) so I settled myself on a couch in the lounge. At the far side I noticed a pair of masculine feet showing over the back of an armchair. I wondered to whom they belonged, but it seemed of little import after the adventures of the last two days. My mind kept reverting to the tombs and the silence, the boy with the bird-like call, and the flea-bitten grey clinking her bit.

III

By eleven o'clock I was in the taxi on the way to Jerusalem. I had a seat by the window, behind an Arab in a dark brown *abayah* trimmed with gold thread. On my left there was a plump man wearing a black flowing garment and a turban swathed with white: he looked like one of the sheikhs from the Dome of the Rock. His son was on the far side, a slender boy in an alpaca suit. Every now and then the boy leant across to offer me grapes and sherbet. I had noticed the two of them at Amman. The father had been wrangling with the driver, flinging his arms about and bobbing his head like an excited pigeon. Behind me, there was a Franciscan brother and a Spanish-looking woman with two small children. The elder leant over my shoulder making comments on all she saw. The younger sat on the Franciscan's knee. Everyone was talking in loud voices – the Arab and the driver, the sheikh and his son in Arabic; the Franciscan and the mother and children in English that had a Middle West twang. The radio blared. I was still thinking of Petra: it was like a dream remembered.

The country was on a grand scale: mountainous and lonely, yet not desolate, its prevailing colour a warm red that made me think of Exmoor in autumn, with outcrops of pale rock and now and again clusters of pines or oaks. There were Bedouin tents, and scattered villages with modern houses and shops that had glass fronts.

Then the road dropped to a valley and followed the course of a river running between the banks that were a riot of oleanders and figs and poplars. A lorry overtook us, with a camel sitting up in it, turning its head like a dowager acknowledging the acclamation of the crowds. Still we dropped – to a flat sandy stretch with clumps of tamarisks on either side. We were below the level of the sea, nearing the river Jordan. The heat coming in the window was like blasts from a giant bellows. It beat upon my ear-drums, dulling my senses. The talk was dying down. Soon not a word was spoken. The child who had been leaning over my shoulder lolled against her mother. Her sister slept. We were in the nightmare world of the Dead Sea, with all about us dwarf mountains, death-pale, and strange in shape: some were humped, and some like pyramids.

We rattled over Allenby Bridge, with the green cloudy Jordan flowing sluggishly beneath. To the south the heat shimmered on the Dead Sea. Ahead were the palms of Jericho and, beyond, pointed and savage mountains, with under them, exposed to the full blast of the sun, the refugee camp.

Then through the wilderness. The pressure of the heat was becoming less; the throbbing at my ear-drums had ceased. The child was back at the window, the sheikh was talking to his son. The Franciscan's voice rose and fell.

We were going up to Jerusalem. The Inn of the Good Samaritan was past. Vegetation was beginning again: at first scrub, then junipers and olives, figs and cypresses and eucalyptus trees. Above a shoulder of the hills, the Mount of Olives rose against the sky. Like many travellers before me, I felt that I was coming home.

CHAPTER XXVI

The Old City

And the end of all our exploring
Will be to arrive where we started
And know the place for the first time.

T. S. ELIOT

IT WAS my last evening in Jerusalem.

As I crossed the road from Gethsemane, through the Valley of Jehosaphat with its crowded desolation of tombs, the clear searching light picked out each mark and crevice on the city walls; picked out the lions of Judah carved above Saint Stephen's Gate. It fell too, like a golden veil on the marbles in the courtyard of Saint Anne's and on the great Crusader church.

Then the sun dropped and stars shone in the darkening sky. Lamps in iron brackets flung a pale glimmer in lanes dropping in shallow steps, mysteriously. Shadowy figures passed and a woman's face stared through a barred window. A fire glowed in a bakery where a man in a white apron turned over the circles of dough with a long oar-like implement. In the shabby, echoing *souk* of Kattinin, steam was coming out of the Turkish baths, and next to them, through a half-open door, I saw a cow with her calf standing in the straw under a vaulted Crusader roof.

I dined with Stewart Perowne and the Poetical Banker in the Dom Polski, in an upper room approached by a flight of outside steps overhung by a vine. A second flight led to the roof. There the night was cool. Sheets on a line flapped in the breeze. The stars had paled now, and the moon, almost at its full, hung above the Mount of Olives, washing its slopes to an unearthly pallor that intensified the solid blackness of firs and cypresses and the metallic darkness of the olive trees in Gethsemane.

The city was below me; the massive walls; the Damascus Gate: towers; cupolas; minarets; plain square houses; streets winding and criss-crossing. The Dome of the Rock looked like a silver flower floating upon the moonlight. Moonlight glinted on the domes of the Holy Sepulchre. By day, in the narrow streets with walls and buildings crowding all about, you hardly notice that the way to Calvary is uphill. Now, with the city spread before me, I could see the Via Dolorosa passing under the Ecce Homo arch, turning sharply at the Third Station, then twisting, bending, backing on itself, and all the while climbing slowly to the church of the Holy Sepulchre. It was as if the Holy Sepulchre were drawing the city to itself: to Calvary and the Tomb left empty.

The city lay there in the moonlit silence. The sounds of the day were hushed. All things extraneous had dropped away. Time had dropped away. I was looking at the Jerusalem with which I was familiar, in whose streets I had walked: a city that, before I had seen her, I had, in some strange way, always loved, always known; so that to come to her was to return to where I belonged, and to leave her was to be torn from where I had always been. I was looking, too, at the city of David and Solomon and the prophets, of Peter and Paul and Stephen. Razed to the ground, ravaged through the ages, she was yet triumphant. Not guiltless, she was holy; the pattern of that other celestial city, the Jerusalem prepared by God himself, sent down from heaven adorned as a bride for her husband.

INDEX